On Moving Well

THE SCOOP-MEISTER'S THOUGHTS ON MINISTRY TRANSITIONS

FOR MINISTERS AND ELDERS

DALE JENKINS

ISBN-13: 978-1986875431
ISBN-10: 1986875431
Published by The Jenkins Institute

Professional editing: Kathy Jarrell
Cover design & interior layout: Joey Sparks

Dedication

Is it odd that I am going to dedicate this book to the weirdest man I know? I don't suppose there is a man I know who has helped me understand preachers and moving and staying over the last 30 years more than Jerrie Barber. I first heard brother Barber preach in Winfield, AL around 1990 and his sermon on "What Will You Do After the Honeymoon is Over" deeply affected me. Then in 1997 when I moved to middle Tennessee and he invited me to lunch to welcome me to town, a one-sided mentorship began that, to this day, gives much to my soul. Jerrie, for whatever reason, sees things other guys don't. No doubt some of the words and/or concepts in this book were first planted in my mind by Brother Jerrie. I jokingly call him the weirdest preacher I know. But that is ONLY a joke. He is a dear friend and a mentor who is deeply loved. It is with the highest admiration that I dedicate this book to Jerrie Barber.

CONTENTS

Part 3 - FOR ELDERS AND CHURCHES

Part 4 - CONCLUDING THOUGHTS

WITH THANKS...

I first determined that I wanted to write a book in 1987 and for the next 25 years I wrote articles, chapters for lectureship books, and camp Bible class material. I got a lot of encouragement from a lot of sources who were very kind about my writing. But a book was not forthcoming. I would dream. I would start. I would create a file. And then about five years ago two people who are superheroes to me emerged.

I am thankful beyond words for Kathy Jarrell and the grace with which she cleans up my scribbling. She can re-craft a sentence and make it say what I meant. She can take it when I am stubborn and she hasn't shot me yet when I've missed a deadline or pushed her to edit even before I get the words she is to edit for me!

Joey Sparks is amazing at spotting stuff I miss. He is officially my formatter and designer of books. He too works fast and he too is efficient. The thing about Joey is that I trust him implicitly. I never worry when he has a change or suggestion. I would let him write words for me.

With these two I can write, turn it over to them, and then forget about it. I am blessed. I love you both, thank you.

And may I indulge myself with one more "thank you?" It is the thrill of my life that I get to work closely with my brother, Jeff, in TJI. Anything that I do through that, we do together. We have to agree to go forward on a project, effort, program. I'm thankful he lets me dream and do and I love him.

INTRODUCTION

In some ways this is the easiest of books to write. It is not deep and full of painstaking theological study and digging into words, and culture, and meaning. I crave that sort of study. I love chapter by chapter, verse by verse, word by word study. I'm presently teaching 2 Peter and a few weeks ago spent a whole Wednesday night on chapter 2, verse 1, the first word there, "But." So this is simple stuff.

On the other hand it is much more difficult. For THIS will, for the most part, be a book of opinion. And when we deal with opinion we are not on solid ground. We might not like the meaning but when Peter tells the multitude in Acts 2 on the Day of Pentecost what to do, it's sort of hard to argue. But, when I suggest a preacher might or might not leave over a matter, that's an opinion and mine could be wrong. It is also more difficult because it deals with what some suggest is the most sensitive area of our work: moving and staying.

So, on the front page. Right here in the introduction I want to be clear: I am human and promise to be wrong some in this book. Please read prayerfully, with discernment, and considering your own situation in these matters. Your opinion may differ from mine. I can live with that. I am not writing to hurt churches or God's men who minister but to help and offer somewhere for them to get started, a resource for them.

WHY ME? Why would I write such a book? Why would I run a thing called the scoop blog? What would make me think anyone would even care what my opinion is on minister moves?

Well, to be honest, I don't know. I just know that rarely does a day go by when I don't get a call from a preacher, elder, or a church looking for a minister or a job or an answer.

It probably started because my dad loved preachers so much BUT to give you a little bit of a more recent timeline, here's the story. For the last 20 years or so I've played a little game with my friend Andy called "Scoop." I'd not been in Nashville a week when I met Andy, son of one of my favorite preachers, Marlin, as in Connelly. And it didn't take long before he would call me or I would call him and say: "I've got a scoop for you." And we'd play an innocent little guessing game of who was moving or who was coming, or for real fun, who would take the most recent opening.

About 10 years ago I started making these things

public with *The Scoop Blog*. What I suspected was right—preachers like to know what is open, who is moving where and, even if they are not "looking," what might just happen to be "out there." As a result rarely does a day go by that we don't hear from two or three preachers and/or elderships looking or asking about a job. And, frankly, Jeff and I love that we get to be a part of that.

Over time we got more and more calls on when to move, what to do when you begin a new work, how to "negotiate" (I don't really like that carnal sounding word), and an inbox full of other such questions. After a while, I realized many of these messages were virtually the same. And while every situation is unique, there are enough similarities that if I could just get them down somewhere accessible, it would certainly save me a lot of key strokes.

I hope and pray this book blesses your life and your ministry. It is my prayer it will help make the church and Her leadership healthier and love each other more. I suppose my utmost desire from these writings is that Shepherds and Ministers will love each other more, work better together, and forge stronger teams to God's Glory and His Family's Vitality.

Part 1
LET'S GET STARTED

THIS IS MY BOOK

THIS IS MY BOOK: I'm responsible for it. I'm paying to have the cover designed and to have it proofed and formatted and my name will be on it. I've done this long enough by now, that I have a lot of opinions, too many, even on books. Here's how I'm going to do this. Some chapters will be a few paragraphs long, others will be a few pages long. I'm not trying to fill a book, but a need. So I will write what I have to say and am not shooting for filler just to have a certain number of pages. And since we are talking about an area on which the Bible says little, preachers moving, I reserve the right to be wrong. And I give you total freedom to disagree with me. I'll even read your emails and if you win me over, In future editions, I'll change what I've written.

I feel very honored that you are taking the time to read this. I take your time and the responsibility to reward that investment very seriously. I don't want to waste your time.

Finally, IF there is anything I may be able to help you with—whether you are a preacher, elder, member of a search committee—let me know. My cell phone number today is (615) 294-1453. That's been my number for nearly 20 years and I'm not planning on changing it. I don't sleep a lot and unless I am asleep or in a meeting or on the phone with someone else, I will answer.

At *TheJenkinsInstitute.com*, Jeff and I want to help congregations be healthier. We offer multiple resources at our website and we offer consulting at no charge. Just contact us and let us know how we might help.

Blessings.

PRAY, PRAY, PRAY

There is no better place to start in hiring a minister than by praying, now and often. That is obvious and you might even think it is trite.

So, let's talk about prayer.

I was in my first work and the Bible class lesson was on prayer. I asked what I believed to be an innocent question: "Why do we pray?" One of the older, and I thought more spiritual members said: "I ONLY pray because the Bible says to." I knew something didn't sit well on my 19 year old ears that day but wasn't sure what. Today I would be better prepared. I think I'd say something like: "Well, that's a good reason to pray, but if that is the ONLY reason you pray, you will not be effective. We pray because we believe in God, and we believe His Word, and we believe His Promises, and we believe He hears and we believe He answers. We pray because prayer has an effect. And, brother, if we don't, we ought to stop praying; God stopped hearing those prayers a long time ago!"

"If any of you lacks wisdom, let him ask God,

who gives generously to all without reproach, and it will be given him. But let him ask in faith, with no doubting, for the one who doubts is like a wave of the sea that is driven and tossed by the wind. For that person must not suppose that he will receive anything from the Lord; he is a double-minded man, unstable in all his ways" (James 1:5-7, all scripture quotations are from the *English Standard Version* unless otherwise noted).

I have a dear friend who believes God reaches down and points us in the direction He wants us to go. He believes that we never make any effort to find out about, look into, or apply for a work, but that God will take care of us and let us know when it's time for us to move. Basically, He will put us where He needs us with or without any input from us.

I tend to believe that we are called to faith and faithfulness and that outside of those, we get to consider our skills, opportunities, families, needs, goals, and talents and try to determine where we can do the most good. For instance, with my language skills (really, the lack thereof), it would probably be unwise for me to try to move to Japan and minister. But with my heritage and training in local works, striving to build up a congregation seems appropriate.

Neither of these two perspectives—my friend's and mine—negate the necessity of prayer. Here are a few thoughts:

If you put yourself out there by applying for a position, there is the strong possibility you will not get the job. You feel like you set yourself up to be disappointed or hurt. Pray. Pray that your attitude will be godly regardless. It won't help in the first week or two after you are rejected, but if you determine to be mature and think spiritually, then what I am about to say will help you. Otherwise, you are headed for jealousy, bitterness, and declining effectiveness. You didn't get the job and you feel a tinge of disappointment or maybe some anger. It could led to jealousy and/or resentment, both of which are unhealthy in the life of a minister. So hear this clearly:

You prayed didn't you? If you prayed as God instructs, then you prayed for His Will to be done. Those elders prayed too. They prayed that God would help them find the right man for the job. And, now, if you believe, then THAT happened. So trust and try to make it a rejoicing trust. And keep on praying.

JUST SO WE UNDERSTAND EACH OTHER

Anytime I start talking about ministers and moving I sort of go into another gear. Sometimes I assume that people know some of the basics about where I am coming from and they may or may not. So, in case you do not know me, let me give you some basics that might help you on the front end of this conversation.

I love the Lord: There is salvation in no other name. That is universal but also personal. I do not know what I would do without Him. I do know I would be lost. His grace has been realized in my own life (which I've found has made me a much more gracious person). My hope is in Him, my life is hidden in Him, it is to Him that I turn for every good thing.

I love the Lord's Word: My belief in the inspiration of Scripture is so basic and pervasive in shaping all that I am and do that it is hard for me to even describe it. Those of a fancy mindset who like big weighty words might say that I believe in the verbal plenary inspiration of the scriptures. That doesn't even sound right to me. So let me state it clearly: I believe the Bible is God's Word. I believe that so strongly that when something it says doesn't make sense, I assume I'm wrong. I believe it so strongly it literally shapes every part of my life. It is my starting point for every issue and my ending point in every quest. Were it not for the Word of God, I would not know God and I would not know my Savior.

I love the Lord's People: Salvation is from God and in Christ! From Day 1 of the Gospel being preached, when God saved people, He immediately put them in the church (Acts 2:47). When a person is saved they are in the body of Christ ((Ephesians 1:22-23; 5:23).

I love the Lord's Servants. I want to see them be effective. I want them to be faithful. I will be an advocate for them and you can check my track record on that.

BE A TEAM

Paul loved the concept of working with others. It shines through as he talks about fellow-laborers, fellow-slaves, fellow-soldiers, fellow-prisoners, companions, partners, associates, faithful brothers, co-workers Barnabas, Timothy, Silas, Apollos, Titus, Epaphroditus, Onesimus, Phoebe, John Mark, Philemon, Epaphras, Andronicus and Junia, Euodia, Syntyche, Clement, Apphia, Archippus, Luke, Caesarea, Cephas (Peter), Gaius, Judas, Mnason, Sopater, Tertius, Titius Justu, Trophimus, Tychicus, Urbanus, Tryphaena and Tryphosa, Sosthenes, the household of Stephanas, Stephanas, Fortunatus, Achaicus, Aquila and Priscilla, and the list could go on but I think the point is clear. While Paul is often called the greatest influence in Christianity outside of Christ Himself, he did not and could not do it on his own. Neither can we.

Let me state this as clearly and plainly as I can. We are part of a team and if you cannot be, get out of the eldership (you are no shepherd but a lord and a hinderance) or get out of the ministry (you will only do harm in every work you do). There are no lone-ranger Christians.

Here's the "Dale's Uninspired Paraphrase" of 1 Timothy 4:12-13, 18. "Not only has God counted me, who is not worthy, grace, but more, He put me in the ministry and the cherry on top is that I get to work with others."

This is sort of in-between the two prime audiences of this book. Be a team. This is to both elders and preachers. Don't be territorial. At some point prior to a man being hired as a minister, there needs to be a discussion where both minister and elders discuss how they plan on working as a team. If either balks on that: buyer beware. The saddest ministry failure stories I have heard are situations where this teamwork was not understood:

One young man said: "They treated me like just an employee. I'm not. I do understand that I work as their employee but if that is all I am, then I'm out of here. I'm not just 'staff,' I am a part of a team, or at least I want to be."

I once worked in a setting where for five years I was invited into meetings and discussions and involved in the work fully. Then it changed overnight when we added some new elders. When I asked about it, one of the new guys said: "Churches in _____ (city name withheld) don't do business like that." I wanted to say, "well, we did and it worked quite well for five years." I would remain there for a few more years, but my heart died that day.

An elder once said: "There is no reason you should know before any other member of the church." True, unless, that is, you want me to promote, support, and push the train. Let me know how the sausage is made so I can help everyone understand.

Elders, the guy you hire will not be perfect. He will sin, he will disappoint...so did the last guy and so will the next guy. Please give him the same grace when he fails you that you would want or you would want someone to give your son were he in that setting.

Be a team.

Part 2
MINISTERS ONLY

SCOOP BLOG
for the uninitiated

Scoop Blog, proper noun
/skūp·bläg/

1. Useful information for ministers looking to move

2. Helpful place for church's to post that they are looking for a minister

3. Preacher ~~gossip~~ "sharing"

4. Place I go every time it updates to make sure I still have a job

Find it at *thejenkinsinstitute.com/scoops-1/*

DEALING WITH DISAPPOINTMENT

It was 1987 and I was trying out for the preaching job in Hamilton, AL. I was 24 and they should not have hired me. I wouldn't have. I was nervous. I called dad. He talked to me about a job he had once gone after and how he didn't get it. I think he thought they shouldn't hire me too :) and was preparing me for the worst. But he said something to me that night that has never left me: "It is more important how you react when you DON'T get the job than when you do." Now, I'm pretty certain that is not a monumental truth revelation for you. But, do you live it?

See, I can be mad, sad, bad, or whatever (thanks Jerrie B), but it doesn't change anything. When I bite into those emotions and keep chewing, it only leads me to bitterness. Again, your anger, your posting in anger, your whining, your "trying to burn their house down" by talking bad about them, doesn't change anything. They could come to me and say "we are so very sorry, we made a huge mistake" and it wouldn't change anything.

So, I tell preachers all the time that the most important question at this point is:

What have you (I) learned from this that will make me more effective into the future?

THE MOST IMPORTANT QUESTION WHEN LEAVING A DIFFICULT WORK

So you had a tough work. You're not alone. Jesus had a pretty difficult one too and it worked out alright. Your's can too.

You toiled and gave and sacrificed and were unappreciated and got burned or burned out. You were invited to leave. You were told to leave. You were allowed to leave. What now?

There are many questions. Most you'll never get an answer to this side of eternity, and I doubt they will seem important on the other side of it. Questions like: Why? What went wrong? Why didn't they talk to me first?

Please, please know I am not minimizing your hurt. I understand it and you can call me anytime you need to talk and I will listen, BUT, for now there is a much more important question that if you do not deal with it, bitterness will creep into your prayer life, it will creep into your family life, it will creep into your ministry, and it will wrap it's ugly roots around your soul and eventually destroy you from within, from your heart (Hebrews 12:14-15).

So, the most important question you can ask when leaving a difficult work is:
What did you learn from this experience that will make you a better and more effective leader in the future?

Ask that. Now, don't answer it dumbly: "I learned that I do not want to work with guys like that." Answer it smart, answer it prayerfully, answer it with hope for the future. You may hate me now because the human heart wants to blame, to be angry, to seek vengeance, to sulk, but if you will search deeper for the lessons to be learned that will make you better and more for The Cause, you will thank me later. Blessings.

OK, LET'S MAKE SOME HOTDOGS

At age 12 I went to work for Steve McQueen (no, not that one) and till I was 18 I worked in one of his places of business. My favorite was a little window at Eastwood Mall in Birmingham where we sold hotdogs. At some point in that business I determined that one day I would own and run a hotdog stand. That day hasn't come, but I'm still kicking. I don't eat hot dogs often, but a good ballpark hotdog is an experience to be relished (see what I did there?). And a hotdog burnt just right over a campfire can only lead to one thing—another one.

All that goodness and I'm told that if I could just see hotdogs made one time and know what goes into them, I would never eat another one. So, I chose to live my life in blindness and denial.

Of course you are now wondering what in the world all of this has to do with ministry. Stay with me.

A few years back we had a rash of deacons resigning over what seemed to me to be the smallest of issues. When I finally started digging into it, I learned that what seemed routine to me was a boulder to them. See when you are "just a member," a good volunteer, people are so very kind and gracious and appreciative. But when you become a deacon or an elder, then people start bringing you their complaints, they start telling you all the issues and the problems. I've seen it crush the spirit of more than one good man.

Now why am I putting this HERE? Because, if that is true of deacons and elders, multiply it times a 1,000 when you are getting a paycheck from the church. To some that means you are their own personal open dump.

Remember the first time you preached a sermon? It was awful wasn't it? In every rehearsal it was 15 minutes long but when you actually got up and preached it it was 2 minutes and 20 seconds but it felt like an hour, right? But you remember the response. You got kisses on the cheek from little old ladies, sincere deep handshakes from the elders, somebody said to the preacher, "You better watch out for your job, this boy will take it." And so it went. Anytime you'd talk, travel, when you told folks you were going into ministry. It was party city.

Then there was that fateful day that you took your first job. It wasn't long till the honeymoon was over and people were coming to you about everything from the handle in the boy's bathroom being hung up to why the elders weren't qualified. And they expected YOU to fix both. You got the biggest and the smallest complaints. You got the chronic gripers and the occasional "off their meds" crazies. Yep. And you got the full blunt of every mistake grammatically, theologically, and fashionably that one could receive. The fatigue from such is unfathomable. How'd you go from being so good to so bad? You didn't. You just got to see hotdogs made.

As a leader, someone needed or needs to tell you what you are going to see is the underside, the underbelly, the business. Hang in there. The best hotdogs are worth it.

At times, even in this little book something you read may be discouraging. Remember, we're sort of making hotdogs here.

WHO GOT FIRED?

No, this isn't how to read the scoop blog's tea leaves! Though I must say I have a lot of fun with it. I get questions like: "Why'd he get fired?" or "I check it every time to make sure I still have a job..." or "Did they really say that is what they want?" Here's a hint on that last one. If you ever see something in quotes that means the posting church either requested it be posted "just as I sent it" or that what they sent was so very crazy I wanted our legion of readers to be forewarned.

There are specific sentences I have heard in my life that once I heard them I was amazed I had never thought of them but they completely changed the way I viewed something. One was the morning I heard a preacher friend say, "Anytime a preacher moves somebody got fired. Either the church fired him or he fired them."

We hear the war stories of how ministers are sometimes mistreated. I think I've heard them all. One eldership called a guy in Christmas Eve (on a Wednesday night). He thought he was getting a bonus or a raise when they called to meet with him that Christmas Eve, but instead they gave him his 3 month notice. Then there was the guy on a goal Sunday, in which the church set a new record all-time attendance of over 600, who was fired by the elders that afternoon. They felt the church was ready for a change. Those examples, and every one like them, hurt, shock, disappoint, and make many in ministry re-evaluate if they want to continue.

But how many more times has a church embarked on a building program during a time of health and the preacher announced he was moving to a larger work? Or he just felt it was time for a change, and he fired the church? How many times has the preacher fired his congregation? Perhaps when the preacher is fired it seems more intimate and personal but it sometimes helps to realize there is another side.

You get to leave when there is a problem, they "have to stay." I remember Eugene being jealous of me when I left one place that had its share of troubles. And he was right. Try to remember that when leaving. Be gracious. And try, try, to not leave a mess. And, if at all possible, and do all you can to make it possible, support the elders when you leave. They are the most likely candidates to clean up the mess you left behind. In most cases, you are only there for a season, they are there for life.

Brothers, leave graciously. Leave Christ-like.

HOW DO YOU KNOW?

One of the top ten questions we get at The Institute is "How do I know if/when it's time to go?" Of course the old comeback may be cute. "When they stop paying you and tell you to move out of the preacher's house," but that's not really the question.

This is a sincere, heartfelt, often soul-searching question often considered in times of frustration, perceived ineffectiveness, or when a guy feels his work no longer matters or is appreciated.

So, how do I know? In a sentence you don't and can't. More on that in a while, but first:

1 - You learn all you can, knowing you will never know everything you should: Every church has issues present and skeletons past. They have things that even the best church diagnostician couldn't ferret out. They have things the elders don't know that are happening and might play out to your disadvantage. And you could move and everything be wonderful, BUT an unexpected event could happen within a month of your arriving and things fall apart.

2 - Even when there are red-flags: Don't ignore them, but remember even the "bad church" needed ministers. Who would have gone to Corinth? But they were a "church of God..." and needed someone to teach them and encourage them. Why would Paul have sent young Timothy to a church like Ephesus where they were leaving their first love? Because, maybe they needed what Timothy could offer. We all want a "good work" but if we define a good work as an easy work, we are making a mistake

3 - Watch and listen: I like to watch how the elders interact with the church. I like to listen to how they talk to each other. I do not really care (well, I probably do) WHERE they land on an issue but how did they come to that place AND how do they handle and treat each other and those who might come to other conclusions. If the elders don't love each other and enjoy being together, that is hard to live with. Of course, you might change that over time (but that is a mountain of a work).

4 - Ask for wisdom: If they are godly they are praying and if you are striving to be godly you are doing the same. Pray for wisdom. Evaluate your family's spiritual needs and, as best you can, how your skills and their needs, and whether your style and their approach match up. Then take the leap of FAITH (that is less blind that it sounds) and JUMP (or not jump).

Finally (though I reserve the right for this to not be finally):

Back to "you can never know." Did a preacher ever move to a place with his family thinking, "this will end badly"? You just can't know. We live by faith and do our best and if it doesn't work out, we live right and trust God, strive for continued faithfulness and it will work out. If you and your wife love each other and strive to teach your children right, your kids will be fine even in a bad work. If you go to a bad work, it can actually pull your family closer together; I've seen it. You just can't know. As we said earlier: You don't know if a move you didn't make would've turned into a great work that you loved. Neither can you know if a move you do make which goes poorly would've kept things from falling apart back where you came from. You can never know how the decision you DIDN'T make would have turned out. So we pray and live by faith.

Remember: "faith is the substance of things hoped for the evidence of thing not seen" (Hebrews 11:1). If you always knew, it wouldn't be called faith.

MORE ON: SHOULD I GO OR SHOULD I STAY?

I positively love the heart of my preaching brothers and their families. As a group I know of no more pure-hearted, selfless, sincere group of people in the world. I am proud to be a part of the unofficial fraternity of Gospel Servants.

There are few struggles that bug us more than knowing how to know when it is time to stay and when it is time to go. Of course, sometimes leaders/churches make it easy for us :(. But outside of those "opportunities" how does one KNOW to stay or to go?

Some have it easy. They never move. They never consider it. I seriously think my father-in-law, in Roanoke, Alabama, holds the modern record. He has been preaching in that congregation 60+ years at this writing. But others (I might say most) are continually haunted with questions of effectiveness: Could they do better, could someone new help the congregation move forward in ways I can't, have I outlived my impact here? Or the other: Could I influence more people toward heaven at another place, do more good, impact the Kingdom more effectively?

And then this statement will tumble out: "I just want to be where He wants." I love that heart. I know I'm strange and all, but I've thought deeply about this many times and for a long time. I've counseled literally hundreds of ministers who have made basically the same statement with regards to a significantly challenging choice or move.

I contend that our hearts have to be more about what He wants. And that if we get that right, the "where?" is not nearly as significant. God made us human-types a people of choice. I get the grand privilege of evaluating and deciding: I get to look at my set of skills and talents (can I learn French?), the spiritual needs of my family (some children thrive in an environment where there are more Christians, others struggle with being needed in that environment; what's best for them?), the responsibility of physical needs being met (1 Timothy 5:8), the people I am most effective with. Then I get to decide where I'll serve.

And the what? He wants: Our faith and our faithfulness. He want us to care for our family. He wants the growth and health of His Family.

FIVE FILTERS FOR MOVING

Several years ago my dear friend Adam Faughn and I did a weekly podcast called, iPreach. One week we talked about staying and moving. We had four guests on and they helped make it one of the more insightful podcasts that Adam and I ever did. Near the end I gave some of the "filters" I have used to aid me in determining when to move or not.

As I said in the last chapter: I have always believed the bottom line is that God calls us to faithfulness and we get to determine where we can best live out that mission. I've always been thankful—and typically a tad shocked (but that's another book)—when a church calls me and asks me to consider moving to work with them. To be paid to do the greatest work in the world, what a blessing that is at any place. Sometimes in our moments of frustration we forget that. So, with that background, here are a few expanded thoughts building on the last chapter:

1. Where can I be most effective? I preach because I want to reach people and impact their lives. It doesn't matter how happy I am or how much people love me or if I "feel appreciated," or if I love the people. If I am not making the most impact I can with my skills, then I need to move. This could be the hardest measure to figure. Sometimes you underestimate your effectiveness and sometimes you overestimate it. You may not be able to fully assess this. For instance when I left Granny White for Spring Meadows, it looked like the work at Granny White was still progressing; why would I leave a place like that for a little place like Spring Meadows? I felt my effectiveness at Granny White was at best diminishing. I still loved the people but the level of frustration was growing in my life and I felt it was time for someone to come there who could do things I could not. Dad left Hamilton in 1966 for Birmingham (the year of the infamous Birmingham church bombing), because he felt he could reach more people in one Sunday via television than in 10 years of preaching in Hamilton. And, I'd say he was effective in that work. For his 43 years in Birmingham, the church averaged baptizing one person every seven days. He always said to go where you believe you can reach the most people.

2. My family: Is this move best for them? Not is it what will make them happy, but is it best. I left my first work because I could tell my Melanie was suffering spiritually. When we left Hamilton for Granny White we were VERY happy and content "in the great state" (maybe too much so). BUT I wanted my boys to see and know of opportunities they would never have the chance to see or embrace in Hamilton (don't take that wrong my dear Hamilton readers, you know I love you and Hamilton will always be home). My kids thought I was a tyrant for moving them, BUT I knew (I thought) that in the long run they would be happier. I sometimes think this is a little selfish. I wonder if Peter or Paul, Campbell, or Stone would have felt that way. In our sometimes "hyper-sensitive attention to our kids" culture, we might not always be doing them or the work we do justice.

3. Will this move allow me to do more for the Lord? Is it good for me spiritually, will I be challenged. When I left one work, part of my feelings were that the week to week challenges were no longer, well, challenging. If I had so decided I could have pulled a sermon out of an outline book and they, because they loved me, would have been happy with it. That doesn't do the work we are commissioned to do justice. We have the privilege of being in a kind of work where we can be challenged.

4. Can I support my family in this move? Some people think it is wrong for a preacher to move for money and I've known more good men to feel guilt on this front than I can count, but Paul's words to Timothy are for us too (a man who will not provide for his own is worse than an infidel). I've "lost big money" in leaving places before, but I figured I could still support my family on what I would be making. I've had offers in my life to make a whole lot more money, but that did not interest me. That certainly doesn't make me heroic, noble, selfless, or wise. It was a freeing time that taught me in a tangible way that money is not my motivation. Nonetheless, I left one church because I did not see where I could support my growing family there.

5. Do I think I can work with the leadership at this place? This is not, "What are their views on issues?" It is rather, are they reasonable people and can I work with them? That is hard to know before you go, but it is certainly essential to try to figure out.

I don't know if this will help any, but it is some of my process. I've learned that bigger is not always better, though it is always tempting. I'd rather be at a growing church of 50-100 than a stagnant and refusing to do what is necessary church of 1000-2000. Big is in the eyes of the beholder and don't buy into the worldly concept that success equals moving up the ladder.

I trust that regardless of the move, if you will be faithful to the Lord, YOU will be a blessing! Sometimes it's a win-win situation, and isn't God good! I could say much more here but will close with this. I have been blessed well beyond what I deserve or was worthy of at every place that has given me the blessing of serving with them. I don't know why, but I praise the Lord for His goodness. I hope you can know that same blessing.

HOW TO STAY

It's been over 20 years ago, but I remember it like it happened this morning. Dad, Jeff and I got to go to Alaska together and conduct a church growth worksop and preach for the Eielson Fields congregation outside of Fairbanks. Frankly none of the three of us are really hunters or fishers, so what do you do in the middle of Alaska? We'd all, of course, heard of the Alaskan pipeline and we were near it. So, we found it. And drove it. And drove it. And drove it. It's not much to look at. Just a big pipe that goes on and on and on. For 800 miles. The only good part of it all was that I got to be with dad and Jeff for a couple of hours just driving and talking.

As one point Jeff or I asked dad, "How do you stay at a place for 30 years?" We were poised for the answer of a lifetime: plans and pointers, strategies and steps to being effective over many years...I hope you too have your pen prepped.

Dad said: "You don't move."

And, having considered it for 20 years now, he's

pretty much right. You move to stay. You plan to stay.

Here are three quick and simple tips for staying:

1. Study, don't stop preparing: Study the Word of God deeply and continually. Never stop learning from the one Book that never stops giving. Study history, study systems, study families, study current events, study people, BUT most of all study God's truths.

2. Recover quickly: I bet you'll see this again and again in this little book, but in case this is the only chapter you are reading I will to give you Dale's axiom for effectiveness in local work: Your effectiveness in ministry will run a parallel line to the speed with which you recover from a hurt. Paul instructs to forgive as we've been forgiven. Peter says rejoice when we face suffering knowing it is then that we identify with Christ. You will be hurt, talked bad about, misquoted, mistreated and mischaracterized. Accept it and plan up front to recover quickly. And, I'd say further, do all you can to keep your frustration from showing. Remember souls are at stake. How sad to imagine that they may not hear the message that could change their eternity because you were upset over some, by comparison, minor slight or hurt. And that, again, is another reason to move forward from a hurt.

3. Remember who is in charge: I give advice. But

I receive it too. And my best advisor is often my wife. One of her gems is "Let the elders be the elders." And she is right. Do your job, support them in doing theirs and don't get in their way or try to preempt them. If you do, chances are you'll be calling a moving company quickly.

Remember, the mark of success in ministry is not going to one place and staying. While there are studies that show our effectiveness increases with tenure (most say your most effective work does not begin until year seven), lengthy tenure does not assure effectiveness. It's better to leave effective than stay ineffectively. Nor is the mark of a successful ministry how OFTEN you move. Some brethren seem to wear their firings like a badge of merit. I heard one guy say that no faithful preacher could preach the truth clearly and stay longer than two years. Uh, yeah, sure. No the mark of success in ministry comes at the end when the Lord says "well done good and faithful servant." Until then, happy moving, or happy staying.

WHEN DO I TELL MY ELDERS?

This is a tough one. Let me say at the very start of this: do not lie or compromise your values at any time. If you feel any suggestion made here is not the best to do, don't do it.

That said, I know of few things that have more potential to sabotage a good work than the elders knowing in advance that you are looking for or being considered for another work. My long experience says that it will not help anything. Preachers do this thinking it demonstrates integrity, that it is best to be up front and open. What I have seen is good men released by a church when they were contacted by another church, they told their elders, and the elders thought they were being played and released the good man. I've seen good men fired and left without a job simply for talking with another congregation. And I've seen healthy relationships suffer because a minister talked with another church and told his current elders.

While I don't often compare church matters to the business world (that's done way too often by some leaders), this is a situation where it may lend some insight. If your elder who works in the cooperate world was to interview for another job and his bosses found out, he would likely be fired. So when they so react negatively, do not be shocked.

I'm not criticizing elderships here. They are hurt, disappointed, and probably feel betrayed. There is almost a marriage like relationship between the minister and the congregation and often the leaders may feel like they are being cheated on.

I want to implore you to avoid what may creep into your mind. DO not under any circumstances use an offer or a contact from another congregation as leverage to increase your pay or position at your current church. If you do and it "works," you will feel dirty, you will lose some of the trust of the elders, and you will affect the future. It will be tempting, but don't do it.

Do not lie, compromise your convictions, or seek to be harmfully or maliciously deceptive.

One more thought here: how wise would it be immediately after you have been hired to discuss this matter like adults? Yeah, I know you're moving there and will never move again. And that may happen but in 99.98% of cases, you will move again. The elders know it, you know it. Why not discuss it while the relationship is good? And, remember, any conclusion you agree upon, write it down.

I WANT A HARD WORK

Caleb is one of my heroes. We don't know a whole lot about him. Yet, he is that rarity of rarities that everything about whom we know is good! In fact his name occurs 21 times of note in the text. My favorite of those is what Jehovah says of him in Numbers 14:24 "But my servant Caleb, because he has a different spirit..."

Caleb only has five speaking lines but one of them is legendary. He made it on what appears to be his 85th birthday. You know how those days go. Your kids and grands and maybe even a great or two come around and you recount some epic story or commission them to remain strong and faithful. What a way to go out? And with Caleb. No doubt he could give a play by play of spying out the land or crossing the Red Sea (he was one of two men living at that time on the whole earth who had seen it) or of crossing Jordan or walking about the walls of Jericho. But hold off. Caleb at 85 wasn't done living. Hear his speech and the words around it in Joshua 14:

"Then the people of Judah came to Joshua at

Gilgal. And Caleb the son of Jephunneh the Kenizzite said to him, "You know what the Lord said to Moses the man of God in Kadesh-barnea concerning you and me. I was forty years old when Moses the servant of the Lord sent me from Kadesh-barnea to spy out the land, and I brought him word again as it was in my heart. But my brothers who went up with me made the heart of the people melt; yet I wholly followed the Lord my God. And Moses swore on that day, saying, 'Surely the land on which your foot has trodden shall be an inheritance for you and your children forever, because you have wholly followed the Lord my God.' And now, behold, the Lord has kept me alive, just as he said, these forty-five years since the time that the Lord spoke this word to Moses, while Israel walked in the wilderness. And now, behold, I am this day eighty-five years old. I am still as strong today as I was in the day that Moses sent me; my strength now is as my strength was then, for war and for going and coming. So now give me this hill country of which the Lord spoke on that day, for you heard on that day how the Anakim were there, with great fortified cities. It may be that the Lord will be with me, and I shall drive them out just as the Lord said."

What I think we love most is he is pushing forward! 85 year young Caleb wanted to do more, he wanted a challenge, he wanted to make an impact, he didn't want everything to be cushy and comfortable. He wanted the hard work.

As a shade-tree sociologist I tend to spot trends. Sometimes it seems some of us who preach vet jobs like we are looking for an easy work. We want a work where we can influence the most, where there is peace, where their aren't many problems, where the elders are strong and solid, where truth is and has always been taught.

Maybe God needs you at a hard place. Maybe He even needs you at that hard place you are at RIGHT NOW! He certainly needs someone there. The reality is THERE is no easy job but beware of trickling into the mentality of "I want the easy job with the good salary..."

By the way, God blesses faith. He always does. He did Caleb's too: "Therefore Hebron became the inheritance of Caleb ... to this day, because he wholly followed the Lord, the God of Israel. Now the name of Hebron formerly was Kiriath-arba... And the land had rest from war" (Vss. 14-15).

7 LESSONS WHEN A "HARD WORK" IS GETTING TO YOU

You may be feeing "stuck" right now. Trust me when I say I completely understand. I've been there. Sometimes it just seems nearly impossible to go forward and you want to throw in the towel. Before you do, do you mind if I share a few thoughts with you?

Our first work was unbelievably challenging. We were 200 miles from home, just turned 20, newlyweds, and working in a mission outreach church of about 25-30 members. Every week was a challenge, I was trying to go to school full-time, work two jobs and present three lessons every Sunday. I attended my first adult class there—and I was the teacher! The people seemed backward (we were from two completely different cultures) they weren't open, nice, or accepting. Melanie's faith was weakened (only time in our nearly 40 years of marriage that I've experienced that) and I questioned if I was cut out for preaching. There was NO energy. I'm not speaking ill of that church or those people. God used them to help teach me some important things.

Looking back I've thought about what I learned from the experience:

1. I believe that perhaps God "let me go there" so that I would appreciate everywhere I got to go since then. We've never since had a lack of appreciation for the places we've been. So, while you may be enduring a lot of junk right now, it may be that you will appreciate everywhere you go from this point forward, as in, "Things can only get better!"

2. I saw it as a time to learn: My question in ANY HARD work is, "What are you learning from this that will make you better from this point forward?" When I talk to someone who has been fired, allowed to resign, or is leaving a particularly difficult place, I hurt with them. But I really want to ask one question, "What have you learned from this that will make you more effective the rest of your life of service?"

In a difficult setting it is so easy to become negative and let that lead to bitterness and such discouragement that you quit. That would only make satan HAPPY! his goal accomplished. And there is always the snowball effect when that is happening. BUT who knows what God might be preparing you for? Who knows if this time of refinement is designed to prepare you to be bold and grand for Him in some other place.

What if Job had tapped out with the news of his

camels being stolen? What if Paul had quit the first time he'd had his apostleship challenged? What I see often is that instead of learning from challenging times we just develop a bad memory toward that place. But if you can learn something great from this hard time you will actually be able to appreciate the difficulties.

3. Grow with your wife: My opinion is that when the work is challenging and you feel lonely, isolated, and under-appreciated, that is a great time for you and your wife to grow closer together. Sadly I've seen it lead to some couples growing apart but what a time to cement your marriage. "It's just us, our family." Commit to growing spiritually as a family even more right now.

4. This is a time to grow your own spiritual roots deeper: Pray for and with your wife and for the kids. Pray for that sad church and its future, pray for joy in the midst of misery.

5. Change your focus: We can become myopic and miss what God is/can do. I've learned in the worst of settings, when we are faithful, God is still at work. I learned that from reading the first three chapters of Revelation. Even in the most challenging of those churches, Christ saw good and hope. Is there one who you can influence who might be a future leader? one who might leave there and influence another place? one who sees your faith in the fog and is strengthened to hang on themselves?

I know you know this, but it's good to be reminded. Listen, it is not all about us. We don't do this for comfort and ease. If that was the reason we were in this we'd go into some cushy comfortable job like defusing bombs! In some ways isn't your hardest work where you might be MOST needed. If all was well they would not need you. Be God's man in a tough spot, like Titus was in Paul's estimation.

Looking back, I wonder if I gave that work the solid effort I should have. Like Paul in Corinth we may not see that God has bigger plans and many people there (Acts 18:9-10). Now, as to how much time is enough, that varies depending on your tolerance level and your family. It was time for me to go when I thought my wife's faith was in trouble. My one word would be don't give it so much time it destroys your faith or that of your family.

If I were satan I would use discouragement. If he can't get me to teach false, can't make me sin morally, then attack me in a way that makes me feel ineffective or makes me want to quit.

I was watching a TV show a while back, it was about movie studios and one of the characters said something I want to encourage you with. "There are too many bad days in the business not to celebrate the good ones." I've been blessed with so many more good ones than bad ones, but when you're in a bad stretch that quote might be worth having on your bathroom mirror.

Brothers, I hope none of this sounds like I'm preaching at you (though that is what I'm paid to do :)). I know many of you are dealing with challenges and some with burnout and discouragement. Please let me know how I can help.

YOU'RE FIRED

"The Donald," before he was "The President," made "you're fired" a catch phrase but, put anyway you want to, those words still hurt. One day as I was getting my hair cut, I watched as the Washington Nationals "relieved Manny Acta of his duties as field manager." How lovely sounding, they relieved him, he was under stress and now he is relieved, though I doubt he sees it that way, it sure sounds nice.

Running *The Scoop Blog*, I end up intersecting with a good number of preachers who are also "relieved" of their duties. Churches don't use that terminology. They'll say "we believe it's time for a change", or "we want to go another direction," or "we are going to give you the opportunity to find another place to preach," or "we're going to let you resign if you want to" (of course if you don't, you're leaving anyway, so it'd be advisable to take this "opportunity").

Bitterness ensues. I've been told that most every preacher will be fired, and thus given this "chance of an unanticipated" move at least once in their ministry. So far, through the grace of God and the patience of His People, I have been spared that "growth gift." Yet I understand how a root of bitterness could spring up.

My barber, who at the time didn't know what my job is, said about Manny "must be hard being fired in front of everybody. When they fire somebody here they call them in a back room, and unless the person says something, nobody even knows until after they are gone." It occurs to me that part of the pain when "we" are "fired" is that it is so public. But then our job is public so that just goes with it.

All of this got me to thinking. While I have never been "fired," I have fired churches several times. But we do it not even realizing that is what we are doing. We do it and try to justify it in ways that if churches dismissed us with the same words, we'd be furious. We do it and then expect the church to still love us and don't understand why they don't understand. But if the shoe was on the other foot we wouldn't understand: "...we don't want you here -vss- we don't want to be here." "We think it is time for a change -vss- we think it is time for a change." "You'll be OK -vss- you'll be OK."

When I left the little church I preached for in south Alabama, I told them an opportunity had come my way that I didn't feel I could pass up at a church I had always wanted to work with (Hamilton). But what if they'd had a preacher they wanted more than me who had come to them and said he wanted to work there and they said to me "we have had an opportunity come our way that we can't pass up" and they'd dismissed me? I figure I would have been crazy angry. When I left Hamilton, I loved the church but was really just ready for a new challenge, but how would I have felt had they said they were ready for a new challenge and dismissed me? I left Granny White saying I had done about all I could do there and it was time for someone else to come in that could maybe move them forward, but if they'd released me saying they thought I'd done about all I could, I think I could have been bitter.

Frankly I'm not even sure what to make of all of this or what I think about it. Maybe it's just my strange mind thinking' I look forward to hearing your thoughts, too. Remember light not heat!

DUN DUN DUN DUUUUUUN
The Interview

You got to the interview stage. What now? What do I wear? Ask? Look for? Once upon a time I had a whole notebook of interview questions and thoughts. Now I just have a handful of what I believe to be significant insights:

What do I wear? First, ask them what is expected. If you can't live with their answer, you probably shouldn't do the interview.

What is most important? I'm glad I asked. Probably the most important overlooked thing about interviews is this: Be you. That may seem small but it is significant. Be you and try to be the best version of you that you can be. If you don't answer truthfully and clearly, if they do hire you they are not hiring you. They are hiring the guy you are portraying yourself to be. Let them see who you are, what you are passionate about, be honest in your answers. If you don't know just admit it.

If I preach a try-out sermon, should I preach my best sermon? Of course you should. That is what they are expecting. If you don't bring your best they are sitting there thinking, if this is his best we aren't getting much.

What should I ask? Well, I would ask anything that might be a deal-breaker that is not obvious. If you have reason to believe they are a church that doesn't believe in the essentiality of baptism then ask about that. But, TYPICALLY, there are some safe assumptions.

I used to have a long list of questions but found that they rarely help much. Here are a few things I DO think are important to know (note that this list is NOT in order of importance):

1. How do the elders make decisions? I need to know the process. Can your decisions be changed? Does every decision HAVE to be unanimous to pass? Is everyone's voice equal or do you have a senior elder?

2. Do the elders like each other OUT of this room? That's important. If they don't, it will not be as healthy a church as it should be.

3. Do I meet with the elders? How often? When am I not invited? I don't have to be in every meeting, but if you want me to push every train down the tracks it certainly helps for me to see the process.

4. How do the elders handle issues brought to

them? Do they lead out of fear? Do they have every matter settled before they hear it? Do they discount a person who has been a trouble maker in the past? Do people with money have more of a voice than others?

5. How do the elders handle criticisms brought about the preacher? They WILL get criticisms about their preacher. That's a given. The bigger question is how they handle those. Do they over-react and want you to jump through everyone's hoop? Do they listen, evaluate, and then choose to act or not? Do they defend the minister when appropriate?

6. Are the elders soul winners? Do they both know the Gospel AND care for souls?

7. What books (other than the Bible) have influenced the elders?

8. Do the elders believe a preacher "tops out" at a salary? Is there a "no preacher should make more than _____ concept?" Believe it or not, those do exist often.

9. Do the elders treat each other with respect when they disagree?

The notes below are from K. H. Queen of *The Washington Post* in an article that appeared January 28, 2018. I do not know K.H. Queen but do know

Gary Hampton who shared this with me. It seems to fit here. I have added some comments to make it fit our context:

Mistakes in interviews:

1. Lying on the application: Be you on paper. Christians need to not lie.

2. Social media blunders: Listen guys, if your FaceBook page is full of political and/or hateful posts about others, if you are always going off on a rant, don't be shocked when that hurts you.

3. Applicants who show up without questions. Did you do your homework? Have your researched more than just surface details? What about the area? What do the elders do? What is the prime occupation of the area?

4. Applicants who won't shut up: Oops, that's me :).

5. Being a know-it-all: "Some candidates think so highly of themselves they're ready to revamp the entire company before they even get a desk," one hiring manager says. 'You can tell in the interview they've already decided that everything we do here is wrong without any context at all. They're jumping the gun and already talking about what they would do to fix it.'"

6. Not demonstrating humility: "A lack of humility often comes along with being a know-it-all. This person won't admit to any mistakes on the job. 'I ask candidates what is the biggest mistake you've made in your career,' one manager says. 'What did you learn from it? What would you do if you could do it over again? I've had people not be able to articulate anything they've done wrong. That's a big turnoff.'"

7. Not sending a thank you note after: I hear preachers who say "I have never heard back from..." Did they hear back from you? Careful here, don't become a stalker. I have been!!!

POSSIBLE MISTAKES IN ACCEPTING THE JOB

Most preachers I know do MUCH right. They are godly, humble, humans striving to be the best they can be and help others go to heaven. So aside from the obvious...pray, be the person you need to be, preach, and continue to study. There are mistakes ministers make in accepting and in the first few months after accepting a new roll that will harm their potential effectiveness.

1. They didn't get agreements in writing: If an eldership refuses to do things in writing it is a HUGE red flag. If they ask if you are questioning their integrity assure them of the truth: that you are human and sometimes you forget things and need it in case you forget. And further it may be needed for future elderships should a turnover occur. If you don't get things in writing and then they fall apart and you believe you have been wronged—and that does happen sometimes—you have no proof of any sort.

2. They bought a house too quickly: I'm fairly sure I'm on one man mission with this one. This should be number one, but I don't want to appear too obvious on my mission. Unless you have a truckload of money and a backup truck just as filled attached to the first truck, DO NOT rush into purchasing a house. Ever since preachers got wise to the "we'll provide you a house" so you won't have to pay a house payment (thereby killing any equity and helping buy the church more real-estate), preachers have been buying houses. But often we rush into it. DON'T buy till you have lived there a year or longer. This helps with three things: It gives you the freedom to not rush into getting a house, time to learn the congregation and get a feel for if it's a good fit for you and your family, and to learn the area and figure out what neighborhood you want to live in.

3. They used the "church's" email address: Yes, I know you are excited about the work and think you will be there the rest of your life; wasn't that what you thought at the last place too? You want your email address to identify where you are? Great, but who does the address actually belong to? You? Not if the church bought the domain or name. There are always some who might be reading your email through the backdoor, it happens. Not that we are sharing national security secrets or anything we should be ashamed of, but some matters of counsel are confidential. And ultimately when you leave you don't want to have to remember to change your email with everyone. And hey, you might miss an episode of *Ministers & Mocha*.

4. They oversold themselves. They made promises they couldn't keep: Be careful about writing checks your mouth, your energy, or your abilities can't cash! Do not sell what you are not, If you make huge claims of all you are going to do: (1) It seems to make your work more about you than God and (2) what if you arrive and find matters that block anything you attempt to do? Be who you are. Express dreams for what you think might be able to be done. Show some excitement but don't assure them, as one guy did a few years ago, "this church is gonna fly, just watch." We did, the guy crashed and burned after 18 months.

5. They undersold themselves, i.e. agreed to a salary package they could not live on: You might believe this is the simple converse of the previous mistake and while you do not need to undersell your God-given abilities and honed skills this is more about 1 Timothy 5:8. You have a fiduciary responsibility to take care of your family. Don't be greedy but DO be honest. If the church is offering a compensation you cannot live on BUT could do better AND you are interested in the work, be honest and clear about your needs and why they are what they are.

6. They focused on only one segment of the church: This tends to happen naturally. When we are younger we tend to focus on and cater to flock with the younger folks and as we grow older we do the same with the older people. Here is my suggestion from personal experience. When you are younger you don't have to try with the younger people and vice-versa. And if you just float down-stream you will not make as much of an impact. Reach out to the older people. Teach the class they attend. Go to youth events, eat a slice of pizza with them.

7. They didn't learn from the previous experience: When a preacher is released I like to ask, "What did you learn from this experience in a positive way that will help you to be a better preacher in your next ministry?" The grief really isn't worth it if you didn't let God use it to make you better! But it's not just when you've been allowed to resign that this is important. I have a permanent file titled "When I Move." In it I keep good ideas from watching other people move with or start with grace and goodness. I keep mistakes I made in the move and how I would/will do it differently next time. Remember, write it down, because you won't remember!

8. They stopped growing: It would be hard to find a worse mistake for any Christian than for him or her to stop growing. How much more true this is for those of us in ministry. Challenge yourself. What happens with most of us is we preach and something at some point works, so we keep doing that thing. That isn't bad but as time changes we must improve, learn more about how people listen, respond, and are influenced. If what we were doing in the '50's worked and it does not work now (not the message) it should not be shocking.

9. They didn't have a mentor to bounce stuff off of: EVERY person needs mentors. One of the prime mistakes ministers make is not having interested outsiders who know them and love them but who do not in any way profit personally from their decisions, and who can speak wisdom into their situations. The know the minister well enough and they trust each other enough to advise them.

10. In the interview they listened to doctrinal stands on issues rather than how the elders/ leaders handled issues and how the elders dealt with each other and with him as a preacher: Yes, issues matter, but there is a real reason to be at least as interested in how the elders interact with each other as where they are on specific issues. Can they debate and be friends? Do they treat each other and those who see things differently than they do with respect? Do they listen or do they think they are smarter than everyone around them?

11. They didn't try out enough! There are several advantages to interviewing a good bit. You learn from each experience and practice interviews your interview skills.

12. They did not follow up: We've written a good bit to church leaders about communicating with candidates. Here's a brave thought. Try to convince elderships who DO NOT offer you a job to do a brief interview with you helping you understand how you could have interviewed better. You can't do this bitterly, but if you really want to be better, you will try to find out HOW to be. Here's the request: I want to be the best I can be, please help me by letting me know what I can improve in my interviewing.

13. They rushed: We'll toss this one that makes it a baker's dozen strongly into the opinion pile. Consider this. On Sunday you preached one of your most emotional sermons, your moving sermon. In it you tried to wrap-up and emphasize much of what matters, you perhaps reviewed your time there, you said good-bye, you challenged them to go forward in faith. It was an Acts 20 moment. Then Monday through Friday you moved. And while physically sore and emotionally spent, on the next Sunday you preach that important and, yes, emotional first sermon at your new place. So, back to back some of your most significant sermons and a move in-between. Here's a thought, see if the church you are going TO will give you one or two Sundays to settle in with pay. The fruit of it will probably be worth it.

Of course these are, for the most part, just my opinions. Your list may be completely different. So feel free to add to and/or make suggestions below.

A DIRTY WORD?

I woke up early this morning. I do that a lot, this morning it was 3 A.M. and I had something on my mind that wouldn't get off my mind. I was to have a meeting in a couple of days with an eldership who was hiring a preacher and he had asked if I would mind meeting with them to talk through money and benefits. I do that a couple of times a year.

But this morning it occurred to me why this talk of negotiating bugs me. The very word sounds carnal and like something a preacher wouldn't or shouldn't do. I feel strongly about ministers and pay and what a good thing it is when we fulfill Paul's words in 1 Corinthians 9 and help a preacher be better than an infidel (I.e. 1 Timothy 5:8). What was bothering me about when preachers work with or I work on behalf of them concerning salary, when I negotiate in their behalf?

It's Paul's words also in 1 Corinthians, "you've been bought with a price" (6:20).

So here's the warning/tweet of this short chapter:

"Never be bought, because you have already been bought."

There will be brethren who think they can buy you. They think they can give you enough money, comfort, stuff, security, and praise, that you will say what they want you to say. Some of you know the look of "we own you."

Listen carefully, you have been bought with a price and no one can match the price paid for you! They can try to buy their truth, but it is not their truth that owns you.

NOW all of this does not mean you can't be paid. This is a YOU thing. YOU believe God's truth!!! Do not allow money to keep you from teaching truth. That does not mean you are not under the authority of elders. If you have them in the congregation you are a part of then you are under their authority. That's not a money thing, It's a Bible authority thing.

Now, let's talk about money.

LET'S TALK MONEY

From my experience with literally thousands of preachers I've noticed that "our" guys are not greedy, money-grubbing, out for filthy-lucre guys. They are humble, sacrificial, talented men who, if they were money-driven, could make much more in the cooperate or competitive world. They will turn down raises, feel bad if they think they are making too much, give you the last dollar in their wallets or the shirts off their backs.

Yet, I'm reminded of one of my favorite lines from one of my favorite movies:
George Bailey: *I know one way you can help me. You don't happen to have $8,000 bucks on you?*
Clarence: *No, we don't use money in Heaven.*
George Bailey: *Well, it comes in real handy down here, bud!*

All that to say: you need to figure out how to make enough money to live and support your family OR you need to adjust your standard of living.

Contrary to popular preacher myth, there is no sin, crime or shame in moving for money. God is not opposed to money. He created all of the wealth in the world, Psalm 50:10 says "the cattle on a thousand hills are His." MANY of his faithful servants were not only wealthy BUT rich. He made Solomon rich, Abraham, women of substance ministered to Jesus, Mary/Martha/Lazarus, JOB "have you considered" AND then he became much richer. More recently: A.Campbell, D.Lipscomb, A.M. Burton and a score of generous people I have known well used the riches God gave them for great good.

My point here is that we do not need to feel guilty or to make others who are wealthy feel sinful that they are wealthy. We should simple do as the Spirit instructed,

> "Teach those who are rich in this world not to be proud and not to trust in their money, which is so unreliable. Their trust should be in God, who richly gives us all we need for our enjoyment. Tell them to use their money to do good. They should be rich in good works and generous to those in need, always being ready to share with others. By doing this they will be storing up their treasure as a good foundation for the future so that they may experience true life" (1 Timothy 6:17-19, NLT).

Notice there several imperatives in that text that outlines our teaching responsibilities towards the rich that will help them with their wealth. Teach them:

1. *Not to be proud. Money, by it's very nature can lead*

us to pride and display.
2. Not to trust in unreliable money. Have you checked
the stock market lately?
3. To trust God and enjoy the blessing of His wealth.
4. To be rich in good works.
5. To be generous to others in need.
6. To be ready to share.

But, back to our thesis. It is OK to make money for your preaching but if you preach for money, you need to seriously consider getting out and finding something else to do for it will be a pitfall for you. You will find yourself compromising convictions to "keep the money happy" and you will find yourself chasing money.

I have a friend who traces the major turn in his ministry to the time when he was able to talk with his leaders, adult-to-adult, about money. Learn to talk honestly about money.

1. Start a file: Call it "When I Move." I have one. It is the only file in my computer that has ever been under a password. Anytime something happens, I learn something, I hear something, I see something smart or useful someone else has done relative to moving, I open it and toss the tip in there.

2. Do not accept a job for less than you can comfortably live on. Notice I did not say live comfortably on, this bullet point is not about comfort but about margin. What I mean is if your bills add up to $1,000 a month and they offer you $950, you can't do it. Now, it is OK, if you can, to adjust your standard of living for a job you want, I've done that. But don't get to the point where you do harm to the church's reputation and find yourself always having to stress over money. I hear some brave hearted objector: "Oh, we'll live on faith." I love it, and God blesses faith. But don't be dumb. Faith is not sight, but it is also not blind! You did not take a vow of poverty when you determined to preach. If the church can do better and there is a need, and they won't, be leery of taking the job. I say all of that knowing that sometimes you have to take the job offered and that you can't name your own salary.

3. When negotiating share why you need $10,000 a week or $1,000 a week. Be honest and open and lay out your budget: I have a medical bill that costs me x, I'm paying x on my student loans, we have a child whose medicines cost x, we someday want a child and I will need more money then, I made a mistake and am paying for it (they all made/make them too).

4. If you can't agree on a salary don't go BUT if you are close and you think it would be a good fit, be honest and negotiate. "I do not want to be greedy or unfair but I need $100 more a week to make this happen. Is that possible?"

5. For some of you talking about money is harder

than going to a bad Thanksgiving Gathering. For you, consider bringing in a closer. Someone who can talk to both sides and say some things that will help make the deal happen.

6. Don't forget to include extras: a signing bonus, cell phone, resources allowance, computer every 2-3 years, admissions to ball games or such events if you are a Youth Minister, how about helping meet your insurance deductible so you can keep your premiums lower.

7. Talk on the front end about raises: Have an understanding and get it in writing. Different people do it different ways. Many ask for an annual cost of living raise. Here is what I do. I ask that they discuss my salary with the possibility of an increase every year and that they let me know they discussed it and if they do not, that they give me permission to ask about it without malice. See, time flies, and before you know it you've been there for 4 or 5 years and have not gotten a raise. And while you think about it every paycheck, they have not given it is second thought and often do not even realize they haven't. I was in a meeting a few years ago and the elders came to me and said: "We feel awful. We love _____ (their preacher) and we realized that he has been here seven years and we haven't given him a raise. What should we do?" What they didn't know was that the preacher had already told me he had never gotten a raise and he thought it was because they weren't please with him and they wanted him gone. But he was not going to go to them "hat in hand" and beg. Amazing, they loved him, and he had not clue. What do we do? I suggested giving him a big bonus, an apology, and a raise.

Money—talk about it.

HOW TO LEAVE A CONGREGATION GRACEFULLY

If you have preached very long at all, you have seen someone leave the congregation that you are a part of. And you know, there is no good bad way to leave.

Think that sentence through and when you're done, come back...

Okay, that was fun. I've seen a lot of folks leave a lot of churches over the years. Sometimes they try to do harm. Sometimes they realize the church has changed, or they have changed, or their needs have changed and they just determine to move on. But sometimes they try to make a stir, create confusion, and even division. Sometimes they go on social media and post something designed to vent, or that is passive aggressive, or just say something mean.

Before we go further I have a question for you. Has that ever ended well? Has it ever caused change? Has it ever helped a church to grow? Has it ever caused the venter to be more spiritual or closer to God? Has it actually helped anyone? When that person, if that person, ever runs into one of the elders or members at the grocery or an area meeting or lectureship, is it a grand reunion? If that person were to visit again, what would people think, feel? Okay, that was more than one question, sorry.

I'll give you time to come up with an answer if you need to...

Now, what is true in general in this case is even more true for preachers. If you leave angry and vent, and fume, and air your frustrations, and try to take down the eldership, or let everyone know how miserably you were treated, or that you were lied to, or that you don't think anyone there is good, or that they don't deserve a preacher...

I will let you know now, it won't serve any positive, helpful, or God honoring purpose. Don't feel compelled to pout, blast, or even to tell you besties that the elders are godless liars (oddly, they were good enough for you to take a check from the week before it all fell apart).

Well, if I can't do all of that how do I leave?

1. Honestly: Don't lie to save face. Don't tell something not true for the sake of unity. It is not right to sin.

2. That said, as my father-in-law says, "You don't have to tell everything you know." If the circumstances are bad and someone asks for your commentary. Tell them you really don't want to talk about it and for them to see the elders. The elders are the elders and they will have to shepherd that person. Be gracious. If the elders lie, they will stand before God for it.

3. Graciously: Don't make a mess as you leave. Why would you? Do all you can to leave things with them having the best chance of going forward in a good way. Notice that the word has Grace in it. Be full of grace as you leave.

4. Prayerfully: Leave them with prayer. Pray for them. Assure them you will pray for them in the future.

5. Completely: Don't try to hold on to them with one hand as you leave. Give the next guy who will stand in the pulpit the best chance to succeed, so when you are gone be gone.

6. Thankfully: Whether long or short there was a time when you delighted in that place. Say "thank you" every positive way you can. You may have to get creative but figure out how to say "thanks."

7. Optimistically: Leave them with hope in an

eternal God. As long as God is in heaven there is hope for the future. Your prayer should always be that the days AHEAD will be the best for the church there.

UNDERSTANDING THE EMOTIONS OF MOVING *or* "FEELINGS, OHOHOHOHHH, FEELINGS"

I can't tell you how to feel. But a solid 80% of you will have some of the following emotions. That 80% will be the ones who made a decision to leave one work to go to another one.

You'll wonder if you made the right decision. I want to assure you, you did. How can I know that? Because there isn't a wrong decision unless you moved with the wrong motives and the wrong motives are not because your family will be happier, or money, or to get away from something that was killing your faith and ministry, or because you thought you were going to be fired, or because you wanted to preach God's Truths to more people. The wrong motives would be for the glory of self, for the opportunity to sin more, or any other sinful reason. I'll assume that wasn't it.

But that won't keep you from wondering. What would have happened if I'd waited? What would have happened if I had said "no" to them? A dear friend told me of driving down I-40, he'd been at his new work for nearly two years and it was going well, and he started weeping uncontrollably to the point that he had to pull over to the shoulder. I understood. There's just something very human about second guessing our decisions.

But you can't know. You can't know what might have happened if you had not moved, or how the work you didn't stay at would have gone. You can't know if something else that was/is a better fit would have come along. You just can't know. You can't know how your children would have been affected if you had stayed instead of leaving.

I have one word for you: "Trust in the Lord with all your heart, in all your ways acknowledge Him, and He will direct your paths" (Proverbs 3:5-6).

10 TIPS TOWARD PRODUCTIVE COMIN' AND GOIN' (WELL ACTUALLY, 10 OR MORE)

As a minister I've always wanted to arrive well and leave even better. As a minister you want to leave on positive terms even if it is not in the best of circumstances. You also want to start well and make powerful first impressions so that you can be your most effective for the Lord. Here's a handful of things I've found helpful in both.

Before You Go:

1. Leave happy, REGARDLESS: I don't care how they treated you, you be bigger. You have God's grace in your life, the forgiveness of sins, the hope of heaven: Leave happy. If they really mistreated you, make them wish they hadn't. If you leave with anger or increase drama, you will not help the church and you will only confirm their distaste of you. You know the church is much bigger than you OR than whatever issue is out there that is causing you to leave. You know Christ loves the church and died for it. And you know that God loves you regardless of how "they" have treated you or may feel about you for whatever reason. Leave

HAPPY. Determine in the best of days that if/when the worst of days happens, you will leave happy. Predetermine now that you will leave happy.

2. Pray for the VERY best: The church is the Lord's, His Kingdom, His Work, and you want it to increase, to be healthy, for the future to be better. In every setting, speak well of His Bride and optimistically of the future. Regardless of the circumstances surrounding your leaving, they will meet the week after you leave and someone will stand up and talk and they will call that person the preacher. They will hire a "next guy" and you want him to accomplish greater things and reach more people than you did. That may just require that you make an effort to be a better person than you are. One of the best practices to help you do that is to pray! Pray for good.

3. Say I love you: Letting them know your care for them doesn't end with your "contract." Just like with people, churches have personalities and some are more lovable than others, but love them out loud. Yes, surely there are people there who are a challenge to love, BUT just as surely there are some there with whom you will leave your heart.

4. Say thank you: It's one of our best words. Look for reasons to say thank you. Make a list, start it now, of all the things you are thankful for about the church where you are. There are multitudes of reasons to be thankful for the church either locally or globally, I made a list once upon a time of 365 things about which I was thankful. In leaving, be overly gracious. Thank them for every good thing you can remember. That's what Paul did even with the experience he had in Philippi and with a church as troubled as Corinth. As I heard my brother say YEARS ago: Remember the best, forget the rest.

5. Evangelize: Note this. Regardless of why you leave, whether on good terms or in a less than good parting, unless you leave in a hearse, from the moment you publicly say: "I'm leaving," every word will be parsed. There will be those who will try to make the elders, leaders or you look bad. You can't control HOW people hear, but you can control what you say. Why not use this time, whether it's six weeks or six months, to preach sermons on baptism, salvation, evangelism, and to reach people you may have influenced?

6. Learn: I saved this one for last because it may be the most important one for YOU to hear. Learn from this leaving. What could I have done better? What do I need to improve on as I move into my next work? How can I reach more people? Can I communicate more clearly? How will I improve on my relationship with the next elders I work with? If you were mistreated, you can either wallow in it or learn from it. And the lesson is not to never trust, never work for, or never put yourself in the situation again—there is more to learn. It may even be the Lord trying to teach you something. Be a learner.

Getting Started:

1. Take a Sunday or two off between your last Sunday where you are and the first Sunday where you are going: Obviously money could keep that from happening, but if both sides (the one you are leaving and the one you are going to) will take a Sunday, or if the one you are going to will give you an extra week, you will be better poised for the new work. My experience is that preaching your heart one week in leaving and seven days later having to knock a home run while moving in between, is next to impossible physically and emotionally. Try to figure out how to live with some margin in this.

2. Post a signup sheet: For good or bad, some people will judge you by if you ever had them into your home. This MAY be even more true if you live in the preacher's house. Figure out how to systemically work through the membership having people into your home. Here are a few starters: One friend invited members into his home monthly by last name: A-B in January, C-D in February, etc. Another did it by areas. One guy who was going to be in his new work before his family (as they were finishing the school year) put up a signup sheet with times he could eat with people, either at their house or a meal out together. Do what it takes to spend some one-on-one time with everyone you can. You will not regret that at any point.

3. Become a historian: When I moved to Granny White they had bound all bulletins dating back to

1953. I read them all. That may be a little extreme, but find out all you can find out about the history of the congregation. It will serve you well as you learn the what's and why's of that community. Learn the highs and the lows and see what they celebrated and what they grieved. Ask long-term members what were the most exciting things and the most challenging things experienced there. Learn about now-departed personalities who were loved (or not) and why. What did they bring to the table that made them effective and influential there?

4. Don't buy a house: PLEASE don't move to a new place a buy a house the first year unless there is a VERY, VERY, VERY compelling reason. Give yourself time to learn the area, neighborhoods, etc. Give your family time to make sure you plan on staying a little while. You'll probably have an idea within a year.

5. Start fresh! It's time to do an emotional garage sale. Leave the hurt behind. Don't mention your previous congregations too often, you're not there anymore. Move forward. A few months ago, Melanie and I had a huge yard-sale. We were amazed to realize that we had unopened boxes from our moves FOUR houses ago! Stuff that movers put in boxes and moved 20 years ago that we had never touched! I think we can do without MOST of that stuff. If you carry some of that stuff with you emotionally, it will only drag you down.

6. When you know where you are going, send the congregation a letter for their bulletin or website, letting them know you are honored to be coming to work with them. Tell them about you, your family, and your dreams. Include your mailing address and email address and invite them to write you and give you some of their own history. You'll know more folks going in than you ever imagined.

9 KEYS TO EFFECTIVENESS IN LOCAL WORK
"...fully carry out the ministry God has given you"
2 Timothy 4:5

Your opportunity to stay in ministry and be effective is in direct proportion to several significant attitudes and actions. I am sure this list is not exhaustive AND that there will be some redundancy in this and my other writings, but this reflects what I have observed.

1. Your ability to move forward after a hurt: This is not a maybe or a possibility but a certainty: if you are in ministry, you will be hurt. There will be people who will gossip about you, who will want you to be fired, who will question your motives, who will accuse you falsely, who will be out to get you. So, the better question is, how quickly can you move on from a hurt? If you can't—if you harbor it, feed it, focus on it, rehearse it over and over in your mind or with your friends—you will struggle to stay in ministry. Move on.

2. Your willingness to let the elders be the elders: The best ministerial advice I've gotten from my wife is this simple adage: "Let the elders be the elders." She will repeat it to me often and she is correct. I should encourage them, give input as wanted, help them grow and seek to help them be the spiritual men and leaders God demands them to be. BUT I must always remember my role is to preach and minister and their's is to shepherd and govern. They know things about the history of the church and the members that you do not. They were probably there before you got there and will be there to pick up the pieces should things go foul. Let them be the elders.

3. Your readiness to work with people with whom you disagree: Because we deal with heady matters like truth and heaven and hell, with unchangeable things like truth and God's Word, it can become easy for you to live in "fight mode." There are going to be people with whom you disagree. Sometimes it will be big issues, sometimes smaller. Unless it is a matter of clear doctrine (and please don't make every molehill a mountain you would die on) strive to work with those with whom you disagree. Do this for the sake of the Kingdom. If you do not learn how to do this, you will spend your life moving and moving and moving and will rarely affect anyone. Learn to see the bigger picture and to work well with others. Let me add here that you have to learn to relent, to back off, and to lose sometimes if you are going to win with the people you work with, around, and for.

4. Your disposition in working with people whom you do not like because of personality issues: While this one is similar to number three, it is a tad different. If we are honest we will admit there are people whom it is just hard for us to like. Often what seems to happen is when a preacher doesn't like something, they try to make it a doctrinal matter. I don't think it is on purpose but it does seem to happen. If you find someone you don't like—whether it is their approach to things, their volume, or simply their personal tastes—learn to be bigger than your personal preferences.

5. Your capacity not to use matters of confidence in your public teaching: People are going to come to you with their "issues" and there will be times you will be tempted to minister to them from the pulpit. If people become aware that you are taking matters spoken in confidence to the pulpit you will lose your effectiveness. Don't!

6. Your decision to not talk bad about others: First off, gossip is a sin. But in addition to that, it will come back to haunt you. Something you say about another will make it's way back to them. You'll fall into a habit that is a bad one. Decide now you aren't going to spend your ministry regretting negative things you have said negatively about others. Love all.

7. Your commitment to preach the Word: Our brethren want, need, appreciate and respect the

Word. If you lean heavily into the Word of God you will both please Him and open the most significant door to your messages being effective. It is also important to remember that it is the Word that quickens. It is where our own personal faith comes from (Romans 10:17). If you are lacking passion in your ministry, it could be because of personal sin, lack of love and involvement in the lives of others, or lack of allowing the Word of God to confront your own soul.

8. How much time you give Bible studies: By that I mean your own private study. Work hard, prepare, read, study! If you don't study, you may be successful for a period of time, but without study, there is no way you will have longevity. If you want to be truly effective, it is more than just your own Bible studies but also the Bible studies you do with others. Study the Bible with those who are lost. The Word will not return empty. Stir the waters, it solves a multitude of problems.

9. Your attention to your own spiritual life: If you take your focus off your own spiritual health, you will stress out, strangle, struggle, smother and sink! Personal spiritual growth will help you handle the impossible schedule and the difficult brethren.

I pray that you will do great things to the glory of God and the growth of His Kingdom.

Part 3
FOR ELDERS AND CHURCHES

HOW TO LET YOUR PREACHER GO

If you are starting in this section it is probably because you are a part of hiring a minister. Thank you for reading this. And if you are hiring a minister there is a very good chance that you are replacing a previous one. And there is a chance that the reason is because you or someone else was a part of helping or allowing the previous guy to go.

The fact is there will be preachers who are fired or let go. And as painful as it is and as disruptive as it will probably be, some need to be fired and some need to be let go. I hope you never have to be a part of such, but there is a strong possibility that you will be. Please pray about it NOW. Don't start praying about it when it has to happen or when you see it coming on, pray about it now, and make a few determinations. Here is a list to get you started:

Communicate, communicate, communicate: I am not sure that overly communicating is possible when it comes to church leaders. I am sure that most leaders think they are communicating clearly but if you ask the members, the former preacher, and the candidates they will all say you are not. Communicate clearly to the guy why he is being let go. Help him grow. Help him to understand. Bug him, don't leave him alone, don't let him wonder. Let him know how to improve. And, it goes without saying (but I've made my living saying things that go without saying), be honest with him. Communicate with him after a month or two and make sure he is coping healthily. If he hasn't found a job in 3 or 6 months after the pay has stopped, communicate with him and let him know he is cared for and help him some more. If you can, communicate with the church why he was let go. If it was just because you thought it was time for a change, there is not necessarily sin in that. But if you can't own that fact publicly and the fallout from it, then don't do it. If you can, speak it clearly, don't leave people wondering. If it was sin, let the guy know you will be communicating that to the church. If he has repented, let them know that too. Be gracious and kind and generous in all of that.

Speak plainly to him before you dismiss him. His shortcomings may be fixable. I know that not every offense is fixable, but if it is and you think you can go forward with him, then give it your best. Talk to him about what is happening and how it might be corrected.

Treat him as an adult. Hopefully he is one.

Be gracious and as full of mercy as you can. Grace and mercy are not just two beautiful spiritual words but they are realities that find their expressions in actions. Speak graciously of him, yes, even if he does not speak well of you. Remember the Golden Rule is NOT "do unto others, if they do unto you, as you would have them do unto you, but only if they hold up their end of the deal."

Do MORE than you said you would. I believe this is one of the most important and worthwhile investments you can make at this juncture. If you promised him three months salary, give four. Unless he has moved out of state, have him pick up those checks in person. It is much more difficult to speak evil of someone you know you have to face once a month. If he is trying to find employment but still hasn't after the severance has stopped, don't cut him off too quickly. Figure out a way to help him further.

Be honest. Be honest with him. Be honest with his family. I know of one preacher who I'm told lied to his family about why he was fired for years. His wife was bitter at the elders when he was the one at fault. Be honest with the church. Be honest with yourselves. Is this just a move to change something cause we don't want to change ourselves or do the really hard work of confronting his adversaries or it is a wise move in what is best for the Body of Christ and him?

Ask if you can do better: With apologies to my University of Tennessee football friends. Phil Fulmer had a couple of challenging years (he was 9-4, 10-4 and 5-7 his last three years), and they let him go. They obviously didn't have a clue what to do next and in 10 years since, they have had four head coaches. Let me be frank. He may not be the best there is, but he may be the best you can get.

Don't throw him under the bus. One of the best ways I've heard of a church handling the "he said" stuff, following a firing was when an eldership considering the young man called to get a reference and were asked why he was let go they said: "Ask him what happened then call us back and we will tell you if that is a fair answer." They let the guy know that was what they were going to do.

Treat the departing preacher righteously regardless of how he treats you: He is a Christian, a brother, and even if he is in the wrong, treat him as godly men would treat another. If he has fallen, don't say things about him that would make it hard for him to correct his sin. The worst thing I think I've ever heard from a leadership, and I've heard it twice, is: "We will be Christians if you will be." Really?

If possible, let him make the call over whether he resigns or is fired. For some guys it will soften the blow. If you can let that guy do that, then do. For others, they wear a firing like a badge of honor. If he feels that way, let him enjoy his walk of shame.

Let him say goodbye. (Unless he's a false teacher.) But let him know if he starts causing division, he will be corrected. Instruct him that he has loved the church, or some in it and he is loved by them and that he will be given the chance to say goodbye and I love you. But again, make it clear that if he goes off script and starts doing harm it will be corrected.

Check on his family. How are they? Let them know they are still loved. Don't let them feel like their dad is a failure. He probably just wasn't the person you needed at that time. Don't let them feel like they are the reason he was fired. I can remember growing up thinking that if I did not behave as a preacher's son should, that dad might get fired for my indiscretions. That was probably a long way from reality, but at a young age that was my perception. It may be that you are just bored with this fellow and want someone different to "feed" you 30 minutes each week. BUT this is his life, his soul! Try to remember that at every juncture.

Understand that there is NO GOOD time to let a guy go. And there is really no good way. Be loving, caring and then do it.

And pray that you won't have to do it again.

When you make your next hire, talk about it in the

interview process: Discuss exits, how they should happen, what would bring them on, and how each party will behave. Agree on these issues before the hire is official. And, put them in writing.

One more note, if I might impose on you. If you find yourself having to replace, fire, hire, over and over and over in a short period of time, it might just be there is a bigger internal issue in the church. Take the time to discover and address the issue. And if that sentence angers you, it may be you are that issue.

TOP 10 REASONS YOUR PREACHER MOVED (THE "I CAN'T COUNT EDITION")

With apologies to Archimedes, here are my top 10 reasons your preacher left. It may be that you didn't fire him, but he fired you. In our research at The Institute here are some of the things we have learned as to why preachers leave:

1. Personal sin: Sometimes we do not take into account this simple fact. He is a human and made of clay. A sin may have "overtaken" his ministry there. Hopefully he can repent, get back up, and continue on. Pray for him. I want to add this thought: could he sin, you know it, and he stay there? Have you unintentionally created an environment where he cannot be human or where he would not tell you if he were struggling to overcome a sin? If so, even without trying, you are contributing to his ongoing sin. I'm sure there are sins that would call for immediate dismissal, but consider it.

2. Someone spread a rumor so widely and viciously about him he had to leave. satan, that jerk, will use anything to harm God's work. And he may use a rumor about God's man to strive to thwart God's plan. I know of a very effective minister who had to leave a work because he fought a moral issue in the town and some immoral person planted a rumor about his life that eventually led to his feeling he had to leave. As the old song goes, "be careful little ears what you hear..." And, please, do not pass on idle gossip.

3. Burn out—he's just tired. Any "profession" that calls on someone to be on call 24/7 is rife with opportunities for family problems and/or burnout. Watch for it. We all get tired but if your preacher can't seem to get his energy back, do something nice for him. And let him know he is loved. Money is always nice, but the fact is a sincere and heartfelt appreciation is sometimes worth more than money.

4. Leadership frustrations: Even with the greatest leadership in the world there are leadership frustrations. It may be that your preacher hit an impasse over an issue. Sometimes leaders get at odds with each other and can't heal. Sometimes preachers begin to feel like we're beating our head against the wall.

5. Well intentioned dragons: I read the book with that title written by Marshall Shelly back in 1984 and the concept is as pungent today as then. Some people mean well but you eventually want to run when you see them coming. Nobody wants to hear a problem or an issue from you every time they are around you. I've known preachers who left a congregation because that just got old. I've also known preachers who left because they were overwhelmed with issues and they didn't feel the elders were supporting them in dealing with them.

6. Not so well intentioned dragons. No explanation needed!

7. Money: He makes too little to feed his family. Yes, he agreed in 1973 to work for $300 a week and a house that he'd never own...but there is this thing called cost of living. If you can't keep up and he has to leave, love him for loving his family (1 Timothy 5:8). If you can pay him more but don't, shame on you! Often elders use teachers pay for their metric. That's awful. Unless you give him the summer off, expect him to preach the same thing each quarter, let him only work from 8-3, give him and his family insurance, retirement, and eventual tenure, it's not a fair metic (note: I LOVE teachers, that is in no way to be offensive to you). Elders, how about this metic. You have children or else you couldn't be an elder. So, ask yourself, "If my son-in-law were offered this package, would I be upset if he moved my daughter and grandchildren there?" If you want a minister to feel that the church WANTS him to leave, nothing speaks as loudly as not increasing his pay.

8. He got fired: It will rarely, very rarely, be stated this way. Most often he will be given the chance to resign. I'm sure I'd appreciate the grace of being able to leave quietly...but it's still being fired.

9. He should never have preached in the first place: We need good deacons, teachers, elders. I know two of the men dad served under as elders for a number of years had preached at one time. They weren't effective or for some other reason didn't continue preaching, but they blessed the church for years in other roles. We need to encourage young men to preach, but we also need to encourage some not to preach but be great leaders in other ways.

10. He was given the opportunity to move: Just as churches sometimes just need a change, so do preachers.

11. The grass was greener elsewhere, or at least spray painted to look like it: Careful here preacher. There are problems in every supposed paradise.

12. He felt he could do more elsewhere. It may be that he just felt he could be more of an influence somewhere else. There is nothing wrong with that. But, preacher guys, remember bigger isn't always better! Would you rather deeply influence 100 people who go to heaven and feel you blessed their lives by helping them see the Savior or minister to more people, but have less of an influence on those people?

13. He felt he was no longer effective there: This is where this chapter started. I've left places not because I no longer loved them or they me, but because I just felt I'd done the best I could and they needed someone to come in and help move them in some areas and ways I could not.

14. It was a bad match from the beginning: Ministry is a lot like marriage. Some folks shouldn't get married to each other. In life, that's a tragedy that probably won't be fixed without sin. In ministry you can part ways and still love each other...from a distance.

15. He felt taken for granted: I don't think there is much we can do about this one. It seems inevitable that over time people will begin to think of "your wonderful" as the norm and get so comfortable or accustomed to it that you no longer feel wanted or effective. Part of this would involve us as ministers considering why we do what we do. Is it for the appreciation or for the Lord. But, folks, remember, everyone likes to be appreciated now and then. The Lord set that example.

16. Family matters: He may be happy as a convertible driver in April :), but his wife may not be. Or his kids may have reached a struggle that precipitates a move. Contrary to some people's beliefs: the preacher's biggest responsibility is to his wife and kids and getting them to heaven."

17. He wasn't encouraged to grow: Listen, your preacher needs mentors he can look up to. He needs retreats he can ATTEND. He needs seminars, books, down times and challenging times. If he does not grow he cannot help you grow. Let him attend a good webinar now and then :). Seriously, he can get so wrapped up in his work and so busy that he doesn't take time or find time or feel he would be given time to grow. Encourage his growth and development.

18. He didn't have any mentors: Encourage him to look up to the right folks.

19. Your elders don't think any preacher should stay longer than _____ (3, 5, 10 you fill in the blank) years: Let me sound like Paul, "Oh foolish..."

20. He doesn't think anyone should stay longer than _____ (again, your blank there): Maybe you could find him a good counselor.

21. He got tired. I'm finishing this at 4:50am. Yep....I'm tired. I'm sure there are more.
God bless you as you strive to care for His servants.

WHY GOOD PREACHERS MOVE - REASON #27

He had been there for nearly twenty years. He was evangelistic. His preaching was still powerful and moving. He was loved and respected. The church had grown. In fact, it had moved into a new building less than five years before. On the first Sunday in May he got up and resigned. It seemed rather abrupt. There was all sorts of speculation as to why he was leaving. Some of it unfair, he got burned out. Some of it coarse, he was having an affair.

It was neither and if people had listened, he told the truth when he resigned. "I love this church and this town, but I feel that I can no longer influence or motivate the church and that it is time for someone else who can to preach here."

If you'd asked the members what he meant I doubt many, maybe none, could explain what he meant. A few weeks earlier he had announced an important meeting for any of the members who wanted to help the church grow. The meeting would be at 4:00 on Sunday afternoon. It was very important.

No one came.

If you'd asked, no one would have said they weren't interested in the meeting or in the church to grow. If you'd told them how deflated, defeated and ineffective no one coming would be, there would have been a large group to come. But he knew and he was just being honest. It was time. He loved them and they loved him. It wasn't a divorce, it wasn't ugly, it wasn't a better job, it was what it was. His deep love for the church made him believe, even though many would have protested, that his time was done and someone else now needed to do what he could not.

Me, I've been there. I'm not sure if he was right or not, but most of us who preach can understand.

No one came. And he left.

ALTERNATIVES TO FIRING

Preacher firings seem to come in waves.

A quick disclaimer or two: I most often hear only one side of the firing. Another disclaimer: Of most of the guys I've known who were fired, I have never heard them preach more than twice, so I don't know what it would be like to hear them week after week. I suspect if I were an elder there would be times I would be tempted to fire the preacher. And I KNOW there are times I would have fired me! I also know that ANY preacher, regardless of how loved he is by the majority of the congregation, has guys and gals "firing" at him (gunning for his job) and the elders get the joy of hearing from all of them, uggh.

I love my preaching friends. I love spending time with them. Lifting up their hands and growing with them are among my favorite things. The whole firing thing is ugly and painful and, while maybe sometimes necessary, I'd like to think some with you about "alternatives to firing." There isn't always another way but here are some thoughts.

1. How about instead of releasing him, help him! What a novel thought. Shepherd him. I know not all preachers will allow themselves to be shepherded, but give it a try. Call the guy in, tell him what you are thinking but that you love him and want to work with him. Ask him if he wants to stay and commit to working with him. Ask him if he will commit to trying to improve. Tell him what he is or is not doing and be specific, don't be vague, we won't get it. "We think your preaching is boring," "We believe you've gotten lazy on us," "We think you have too many illustrations," "We think you've gone sour and negative." Ask him if he understands and if he wants to stay.

a. Is he lazy? Tell him so! Tell him what that means. He may not understand the work expectations from that specific congregation or he may have not had a good role model of a healthy work ethic. Talk to him. Help him learn to keep a schedule. Let him know specifically what is expected of him as your preacher.

b. How about sending him somewhere to learn? We are preachers and we need to improve our skills. If the guy is just boring (a rather relative term; no, don't send me comments saying, "Yes, Dale, I know your relatives are boring."), send him to learn from some guys who aren't boring. This is time to retool. How many jobs REQUIRE continuing education hours? Why would one think that there is no such need for those of us who preach? I am NOT promoting here, but check out The BETTER Conferences. Offer help: We want you to go to two seminars on preaching or public speaking in the next six months. We want you to read a book a month on the art of preaching. We want you to be mentored by _____ once a week over lunch and discuss the public proclamation of the Word. We will pay for this. Let me tell you, it's a WHOLE lot cheaper and less traumatic than a preacher scandal. While I am in no way the model, I do try to attend at least one seminar every year (not lectureships, I do that too) to improve the skill of preaching, because I want to be better at what I do. I find someone who is excellent at standing in front of people and delivering a message and learn from him. I want to know how he communicates, how he puts his material together, how he studies, how he connects.

2. Give him some time away! It is very possible the guy is just exhausted, overwhelmed, or didn't have time to recover from a previous event. Even God rested on the 7th day. Jesus took time away with His disciples to rest. How many times have I heard some elder or member say, "He used to be good. I don't know what happened?" I DO! He is carrying every burden of every member in the church on his shoulders and into the pulpit. Preaching is emotionally draining and ministry is 24 hours a day. It cannot be "left at the office" like a professional counselor who "leaves his clients" at the office. These are not clients, they are souls and Family. If he is getting rough around the edges, give him a few weeks away, even a couple of months away, with pay, and let him recharge. Make him turn off his cell phone one or two days a week. I know of several cases where guys were let go after they had been at the congregation fifteen years or more. They were just done, spent, exhausted, and burned out!

3. Realize the grass may not be greener in another pulpit: As true as it is for the preacher, it may also be true for the church. If you fire this guy you will bring in another one. He too will have "issues" and present challenges. Churches often become like people we've seen who jump out of one relationship and into the next without even thinking! Seriously consider what your expectations are and if they are reasonable. No one can fulfill all of the expectations of every member. Identify which expectations are most significant in your congregation's situation. So, instead of firing, why not fix the preacher/church relationship you are in? Note to preacher guys: if they fired the previous guy for no real reason, you'd better consider that before accepting the job.

4. Listen to him: Find out why he's turned negative or why he's lost heart, or why he's whatever. You may learn a little about yourselves and your leadership that you did not want to know. Sometimes preachers lose heart and energy for a work because the leadership has not led, or has stepped on every idea they've suggested for church health, or they perceive the leadership has lost its heart, or they have just gotten fearful and that has made them ineffective. He may be hurt because what you told him you would do during the interview (i.e., courting) process is not what you are doing. He may be dealing with a family issue that he has been afraid to tell you about. He may be struggling with a sin, that if he gets it off his chest, and you will love him through it, he can be transformed by the grace shown him. He may be ready to move and this meeting may help him talk about it. He may be carrying so many people's burdens that he feels he can hardly go on. And as I said earlier, he may just be worn out and exhausted and need a break.

5. Be patient. Give him 48 or 72 hours to think your proposal over when the meeting is over, and then listen to his suggestions.

6. Do him a favor, tell him the truth. It may be he needs to bless people with other skills God has given him. Years and years ago my friend Diane asked, why won't somebody tell some guys they just shouldn't preach? I know some incredible blessings in congregation where one or two of the elders were preachers and decided they could be more of a blessing shepherding ministers than being preachers. If you try this, he may reject anything you say but at least try. You might end up helping him be a better preacher or a better person.

Maybe one more note here. Let's be honest about it preachers, we've all "fired" more congregations than we have been fired from. When we leave one place for another in the churches eyes it is pretty much us firing the congregation.

HIRING A PREACHER

There is a myth out there that the average tenure for a minister in churches is 18 months to two years. I've been a little suspicious of that number for years because I have hundreds of friends who preach and really can only think of one that has moved every 2 years or so. Our (TJI) studies say the average stay for a preacher is in the five to seven year range.

Furthermore, most studies say that most ministers are more effective AFTER the seventh year of ministry in a specific work. Think about it, most of the larger and more effective (not necessarily parallels there) ministries can be traced to a long tenure of one minister. Name a church that grew strong in a string of revolving door ministers and I'll buy you a—well, I won't buy you anything—but you can take a picture of the shocked look on my face! It just doesn't happen.

Mega-researcher Thom Rainer, author of "*Surprising Insights from the Unchurched*," reveals that the decision of who a church hires to stand in its pulpit is one of the most evangelistic decisions it can make.

Running *The Scoop Blog*, I get to see and hear a lot about preacher hirings and firings. One axiom I propose is: leaders typically hire a new preacher who is not like the previous preacher (let's call is Dale's Axiom for Diminishing Intelligence). Follow me? If the previous guy was known as studious spending a lot of time in his office studying, the preacher who follows him will typically be a guy who is more gregarious and out among people. If the guy carries himself with age and maturity they will follow him by looking for a guy who is energetic and at least appears more youthful. They want a guy not like the previous guy. And it's understandable. As church leaders you hear most from the people who complain. People complained that all he did is study, they didn't compliment his community involvement, or vice-versa. So when you hire the next guy you get a guy who is out and about, not as bookish. OR the previous guy didn't prepare well was the chorus of complaints so you hire a fellow who is a real people person. You'll hear the complaints you'll tend to react to them. So, even if you were pleased, it takes a strong leader not to react to all that he hears and the metric becomes "we want a guy different than the previous guy in _____."

But here's the shocking thing. The new guy will be compared to the previous guy or the one before who did well, AND he never measures up. Because...

he...can't. He is the opposite of that guy!

Do a little analysis of what often happens. The preacher gets tired of hearing complaints as the encouragers more and more take him for granted and he leaves. Or the elders put pressure on him to leave, either by stone-walling on his ideas, leaving him out of the loop, or not even considering cost of living raises. Eventually he "gets the message," or there is a blowup and he leaves. So the elders look for a guy who is DIFFERENT from him. They bring the new guy in and the members complain that he is different.

What a sad merry-go-round. We need to figure out how to work together, how to encourage longer tenures that seem to lead to healthier and more stable congregations, and how to encourage our ministers who love and respect and strive to live and faithfully speak the Word of God. We need to figure out how to help them in the areas they need to improve.

It's not all preachers, it's not all elders, it's not all members fault, but we would do well to plan to love each other, to plan to work together.

I didn't write this, a good friend who preaches did, but I thought elders might want to hear a voice other than mine on this subject.

PREJUDCIES WHEN HIRING A PREACHER

By Anonymous

Every congregation has gone through the process of appointing elders. Since the Bible does not specify a method for selecting elders, each congregation is free to use whatever method they deem appropriate. They are not free, however, to design their own set of qualifications for each potential elder—the Bible gives the standards (1 Tim. 3:1-7; Titus 1:5-9; 1 Peter 5:2-3). Most Bible-believing, book-chapter-verse congregations would not dare appoint a man to be an elder who did not meet those biblical standards; and they would not add qualifications that are not listed in Scripture.

Unfortunately, many congregations would not hesitate to create arbitrary, non-biblical standards for selecting their next preacher. Does the Bible require preachers to be married? No, but many churches will say that their preacher must be married. Does the Bible say that a man must have a graduate degree to preach? Of course not— seminaries and accredited Christian colleges were unknown in the first century. Yet, some churches will only hire a man who has one of those degrees. What about a preacher's family? Many churches not only want their preacher to be married, they want him to have children, or, as it is usually stated, he must be a "family man." I even saw an advertisement for a preacher that stated that he needed to be "between the ages of 35 and 40." (I wonder what they are going to do when the man they hired turns 41.)

Why is this the case? When I asked that question over the years, I usually got a response like this: "Well, churches have their preferences. Some want a younger preacher. Others want an older man. A single man would not be able to preach about marriage like a married man could. They can only hire one man, so they must narrow the list of candidates some way. Again, it's just a matter of preferences."

So, before a congregation ever speaks to a preaching candidate, the church assumes they know his beliefs based on where he went to school. Instead of searching First and Second Timothy and Titus for qualifications for preachers, the church makes an arbitrary list of qualifications that instantly disqualifies men who are otherwise biblically qualified. It seems like many churches are more interested in finding the right resume' instead of finding the right preacher. They prefer what's on paper to what's in the pulpit. They want a politically-correct directory picture, which features the right-aged preacher—who graduated from the right school—with his right-aged children and his right-aged wife. They prefer the stereotype of what the "right" preacher should look like instead of the right preacher.

I have been told that this is just the way it is. In other words, preachers should conform to the standards or be limited in where they can preach. Get the wife. Get the degree from the right school. Have the kids. Don't get too old. Hurry up and get older if you are too young. His ability as a preacher is one thing, but churches give the impression that the marital status, academic credentials, etc. are what matter most.

How did we get here? There are many obvious reasons. Here are a few:

1. **Rising salaries.** Thankfully, churches have recognized that for generations preachers were not compensated appropriately for their work. Some congregations even prided themselves on how little they paid their preacher. If he had extra money, it meant he was preaching for the wrong reasons. That belief is fading, and churches are dedicating much higher percentages of their budgets for the preacher's salary. But if they pay more, they expect more—more education, more experience, more everything.

2. Greater demand for each preaching job. It is not uncommon these days for a church of over 200 members to get 50-75 resumés when their pulpit is open. It is easier to expect more from preaching candidates when a church has so many options.

3. Tradition. When many churches ask, "What do we want from our next preacher?" they answer the question the way they have heard other churches answer it. Most of the advertisements for preachers in brotherhood periodicals look the same. Churches imitate each other.

4. Churches have made the preaching search much more complicated than it should be. A church should ask, "Is he a member of the church? Does he preach the 'whole counsel of God?' Does he communicate the good news of Jesus better than any other man who has shown interest in this job?" Once those questions are answered, the right man for the pulpit will emerge. But as it is, churches tell capable, faithful men who do not meet the extra-biblical standards that they need not apply. "You are a great preacher, but you did not check all the boxes we created." What a shame.

If we are to "speak where the Bible speaks, and be silent where the Bible is silent," then we should also avoid discriminating in areas where the Bible does not discriminate. If a man can preach like Paul, then he should be allowed to have the same resume' as Paul, which included a shameful past and declining health and excluded a wife and children.

Let's encourage faithful men to keep preaching. Let's not put unnecessary barriers in their way!

JUST A THOUGHT

It seems hardly a week goes by that I don't hear of a preacher being "fired," "let go," "allowed to leave," or "given the opportunity to find another place" (incidentally, those all mean the same thing). I imagine elders are trying to spare our feelings but it seems rare that when we are "invited to move" (You know the old joke: "I keep getting invitations to move...as soon as one comes from someone outside our congregation, I may take it.") that we either get the message and/or are told why.

So, "we think you are more boring than watching turtles mate" becomes "we just need someone to help us get our spark back" or "our attendance is down and it has to be someone's fault (other than ours, of course)" becomes "we just think it is time for a change." It's like a bad high school breakup, "It's not you, it's me," or "We'll still be friends," when they mean, "I can't stand being around you and wish you'd drop dead" (No, I've never experienced this, what makes you think otherwise?).

Most churches seem to love the "tryout" sermon, or at least seem stuck on it. It is fraught with all sorts of potential for failure. It ends up being more of a beauty pageant than anything else (I heard one lady say, "he was a good enough preacher, but I didn't like his teeth." His teeth? Really. Man, I wish Paul had said, "preach the Word, be instant in season and out of season, brush your teeth..." Note to potential preacher candidates: I am not advocating a position of not brushing your teeth, if you think I am, you miss the point. Brush your teeth, no one wants to smell your coffee breath!

So instead of a man's ability to expand on, explain and exegete the scriptures we end up relying on the guys ability to comb his hair, groom his kids, and have ONE good sermon. What preacher doesn't have ONE good sermon?

This is disaster waiting to happen. After all, you've heard my best sermon, it's all down hill from here. I heard one guy say, "I don't preach my best sermon during a tryout..." And I wondered what else he lies about! I mean, wouldn't it be just stupid to not preach your best. It'd be like an photographer saying, "Man, I've taken some super pictures, but I don't think I'll put them in my portfolio, I don't want to get people's hopes up."

To those of you hiring a preacher, here's the suggestion: Call the guy, ask for sermon tapes/CDs/DVDs/Links of three random specific dates over the last four months (i.e. January 31, September 7, November 7) and then listen to those. If he wasn't there one of those dates, that may be good too, you may hear what others say about him when he's gone. Or you may want to go after the guy who filled in for him.

After you hear him and after you interview him, either bring him in or just make a decision. Never, NEVER bring a guy in to preach a "tryout sermon" if the elders might not want to hire him, can't afford him, or haven't interviewed him alread. Incidentally, I've seen all three of those happen.

Elders, get as much input as you want but you make the hire. After all, those folks who "want to be involved in the process" will run into the woodwork like roaches when the light comes on if it comes time to fire him. It doesn't matter who hires him, if a change has to be made, you elders will be the ones to do it (Did I say one point? This chapter has officially been hijacked).

NOW HIRING

Since running *The Scoop Blog,* I seem to talk to at least one preacher and one eldership every day and some of what I hear is amazing for any number of reasons.

Few things are as hard to figure out as the rhyme or reason to how churches hire preachers. Few churches have to go through this task every year or two as they did in the past, and that makes the process both more difficult and more important. If you were only hiring for a year and you made a mistake, well, you'd have another chance to fix it not long after the mistake. On the other hand, if you were doing it every 18 months or so, you'd have the experience of how to or how not to hire a preacher.

I seem to get more and more calls from elderships needing help on "how to do it."

So here are some "filters." Leaderships often do themselves a great disservice with filters. What are filters? Elders will often say "we don't want a man who is _____" (under age 40, over age

55, single, has no children, hasn't worked with an eldership before, looking for a job, not looking for a job, was ever fired, etc). With these often "hard" filters a church will sometimes miss their best candidate.

Wouldn't it make more sense to seriously consider people based on them as individuals? I mean, if you wouldn't hire anyone under age 40, you wouldn't have hired Jesus Himself. If you wouldn't consider anyone single, you wouldn't hire the Apostle Paul. It is often that person just below or above the filter age-wise who ends up doing the best work for a congregation. I don't know how often I've heard stories of churches who took a little risk and received the greatest of blessings and had some of their best days as a result. Yes, it will be a lot of work, but it will be work that is rewarded and if you aren't willing to put in a lot of work what kind of leader are you anyway?

In looking for a preacher, find the person. Then go after him! Don't just settle, do the work, find out how to hire that man, and go get him.

Here are a few tips on hiring:

1. The first rule (of course after bathing the situation in prayer) is to determine you are going to do your work well. AND to be done well, it will require some hard work. Yeah, I know some people believe that any Christian man should be able to work with any congregation ... and there are also people who believe the lunar landing was a hoax!! Determine to find the person who is a good fit and match with your congregation. Determine to make contact with every person who contacts you...trust me, it won't be that hard. Call, listen to sermons, do a phone interview. And then...pray once more. Like it or not, who you hire will be major in determining your future!!! Even if he comes for a year and leaves it will affect the church in major ways.

2. Communicate, communicate, communicate: Yeah, I'm a broken record, I know. Determine at the start of this process that "we are going to communicate". If you get a resume, acknowledge it. If you exclude a candidate let him know. If a guy is still "in the hunt" communicate that to him at LEAST once every three weeks. If you tell a guy you'll call him, call him. And the same with the church, keep them posted on where you are. People do not like walking into dark rooms, turn the lights on! So let the people who you talk to know what is going on. Keep him posted! You aren't doing anybody any favors by not. He doesn't want to go there if you don't want him, he just wants to know what's happening. And, when you decide who you are going to hire, let the other guys you've talked to know it. They want God's best for the congregation and if they are not "it" then they will be fine, but don't leave them wondering.

3. Major deal here: DON'T dare bring someone in and let them preach unless you are sure you can work with him! I know he's Sister Bertha's brother's son's neighbor and she says he's great, but don't do it. You have a mission. I heard of one church that did something like that and the church fell in love with the guy so when the elders sat down with him they were $20,000.00 off from what he was making and wasn't looking to move for less money. The church got mad because the elders didn't hire the guy they most wanted. It'd be like test driving a Corvette when all you can afford is a Yugo (Google it). If he is not a guy you can respect or will not respect you, don't bring him in. Here's what I'd suggest: Talk to everyone you can, shoot for the stars, narrow it down to two guys (or three at most) who the elders KNOW they can work with, THEN bring both those guys in for two Sundays each (one Sunday assign them the same text or topic and the other let them pick the one they want) and let the church vote on which they want. That way the church gets their voice in it, but you know he's someone you can work with.

Maybe another note with this one: I'm not a fan of search committees. I know it involves everyone, blah, blah, blah. But if you as an eldership are so out of touch with the members that you don't know the church's needs or are so mistrusted by the members that they won't accept your leadership, RESIGN. Or at least retool! Listen, you'll set his salary, you'll write his job description, you'll call him in when he needs to be disciplined, you'll be the ones to fire him if it comes to that; you should be the ones who hire him! Seek all the input you can and I'm a powerhouse believer in involvement, but ultimately if you aren't willing for the buck to stop with you, then get out!

4. Check references: Duh. Yeah, I know he seems nice, but who doesn't behave well on a date? A couple of notes on the references. Discount one bad reference! Most of us have at least one elder who would give us a negative review. It may say more about the person you are checking with than the candidate. If someone is very quick to criticize the candidate, that should probably tell you something. I know some churches that won't hire a guy if he has been fired. That can cause problems; I've been told that every preacher is fired at least once. So check references, ask questions, and listen.

5. Find the qualities and skills the church needs: I've noticed that most churches just hire guys who are strong in the areas where the previous guy was weak. I understand that. But what if the areas where he was strong were key to something important. I'm not nearly as good at visiting people who are shut-in as I need to be. It's been a struggle all my ministry to do that well. I know the importance of it for some. I worked with a church once where the previous preacher was GREAT at that but I was stronger in some areas where he looked weak. It was a struggle a real struggle. I often wondered if the elders wished they'd checked that out before they hired me.

6. Find out how the guy handles the positions he holds: Yes, I know the doctrines he holds are important, but you will not be able to discuss every issue that might come up or might become a problem in the future. And, God forbid that you come up with a credal sheet that tries to do that (sorry, forgive me for that one–it slipped out before I could pull it back in). You need to know how he deals with it when he doesn't get his way, if his position is different from the elders', and how he handles disagreements. Does he study or just take a cookie-cutter position? Will he learn or did he set his position as if inspired years ago and has never changed a single one? If you line up on 99% of "the issues," and he burns the building down or splits the church on the 1% he sees differently, he is not your man. Trust me on that.

7. Oh, and while I'm up here on this soapbox one other thing: tell the guy what your plans are! Let him know, "We think we will hire the first person we find that we like," "We are going to try out five guys and then hire the one we like best," "We are going to try out five guys and if we don't like any of them we will try out five more," "We are going to narrow it down to two and then let the church vote," "It will probably be three months before we get back with you," "We don't have a clue how to do this or the process we'll use."

OK, I'll climb down off this thing now. I could say so much more on this subject, stuff about praying with the guys you are talking to and helping them see their strengths and weaknesses, about integrity and honesty, about dealing with each other lovingly, but for now I'll sign off.

MISTAKES CHURCHES MAKE IN HIRING

I have the highest respect, love, and admiration for those who serve the Lord and His People in the significant role as an elder/shepherd/overseer. My dad, granddad, and my father-in-law, and his dad all have served in that role. Some of my dearest friends are elders and some of my most significant mentors. So know that none of this is written with an ounce of disrespect.

But sometimes elders make mistakes when it come to hiring ministers (I figure they know it and would admit to these innocent errors). Perhaps this will be of some help to some overwhelmed shepherd out there.

They don't make a mistake of not praying about it. They don't make the mistake of not wanting the best man they can get, but there are still some things that can derail a good hiring process. Here is my top ten list of things I've seen through the years:

1. They did not treat the previous preacher right: Like it or not, preachers talk and even if they didn't, word gets around and if you develop a reputation of not treating preachers right, it will become increasingly difficult to get good guys to want to deal with you. And you ought to understand it. Would you move your wife and/or kids to a place where you and they were going to be mistreated by brethren. How do we "treat a preacher right?" It's actually pretty simple. As an elder, you are a parent so you'll get this: treat him the way you would want your son, your daughter's husband, the father of your grandchildren treated. If you identify areas that give you pause, then correct them.

2. They did not cast a large enough net: OK, as the "creator and prime care-taker" of The Scoop Blog I am both baffled and amazed when I hear about an opening for a minister and then am told, but they don't want it on the blog. Really? So you want the best man you can get, you have prayed that God would help you find him, but you don't want to put the info in a place the best guy you are asking God to help you find is looking? If I were hiring a minister I would want as many resumes, names, and choices as I could get. What is it? You don't want to take the time? You don't want to work that hard? Are you serious about the role you accepted?

3. They did not make an offer when they found the right guy: Processes are good and helpful. And sharing/communicating that process is great. In fact, as I've said, the MORE you communicate openly and honestly throughout the whole process the better. BUT, when you find your guy...HIRE him. Let the other guys know you did it but HIRE the guy. If he is the first guy you talk with, and all the elders are in agreement, HIRE the guy. If he's not the right guy, wait, communicate and wait! But make the hire when you find the guy.

4. They were not willing to do a little more: This is not home finance 101 and I know you have a budget, but if you find the guy you want to hire but are a little away from what he needs to support his family figure out how to pay a little more. Don't let a small percentage keep you from getting the guy you want. And don't expect him to take less for the honor of being your preacher. If you don't think you can do it with the present contribution go to the church and explain, "here is the guy we think can bless us and be a good fit but we need to increase our giving a little to make this happen. Do you all think we can make that happen?" You'll probably be surprised at the result.

5. They did not GO after the guy they knew they wanted: This is a slight twist on #3. If there is a guy you would like to have as your preacher, at least contact him and let him know about the opening and try to get him. You never know. I remember dad saying, "You can hire any preacher on a Monday, you just have to find the right Monday." So you'll never know unless you ask.

6. They set "hard core" rules that excluded the potentially RIGHT guy: I'm not talking theology here but anytime I get a "new listing" of a church looking for a minister and it has a bunch of "the guy must be's..." I see trouble. The best preacher for you might be 27 but will never contact you if you say we are looking for a man between ages 30–45. Or the best guy may not have a degree from a Christian college or be married or have school aged children. It's fine to say you'd prefer ... but when you put it in concrete, you close a lot of doors that could lead to "your best next preacher." Of course, you have that right, but I'd caution you against being hard-core on this.

7. They hired reactionary: It is my experience after doing this for over 20 years that some churches hire in reaction to their previous preacher. And it is understandable but should be avoided. It's understandable; throughout the previous preacher's ministry all they heard were the complaints from those dissatisfied with him. You rarely hear from the folks who loves him. So, if the guy was great at visiting and not as great of a student, the next hire will inevitably be more bookish. If the guy was older and moved slower, the new guy will be younger and excitable. The problem with that is it does not consider the previous guys strengths or what the church LOVED about how he did what he did.

8. They sold more than they are: Listen, you don't

want a guy and wouldn't hire a guy who lied on his resume, who made it look like he was something he is not. Why would you lead him to believe there is no problem when there is one? It's OK (in fact, great) to be the best version of you as you can be, to put your best foot forward but don't be dishonest to him. If you are it will sour the relationship pretty early.

9. They thought one guy could do it all: Don't hire a preacher to "do your Christianing" for you! Folks if the last 50 guys couldn't "grow your church to 1,000" the next guy probably can't either. I remember a dear elder telling me a week after they hired me once upon a time, "We'll be over 1,000 in attendance in 3 years." He was flattering me and what he thought my skills were. BUT I felt deflated, like if it didn't happen was I failing?

10. They did not check enough references: I am absolutely amazed at the number of elderships who do not call references. Some do, but do not ask the right questions. Find out as much as you can about any guy you plan on bringing to preach God's Word to His People. Here's a great question to ask: What have we not asked that we should have?

Let me close similar to how I began this post: I am thankful for elders and for their hearts and great responsibility and how every elder I have ever met wants the best for the Kingdom. Pray for these men and strive to encourage them, not merely compare them to difficult ones you may have encountered. Respect the burden they carry, and you will contribute to that only with joy.

WELCOMING THE NEW GUY

You've done the hard work of finding "the guy" and securing him. Is there anything we can do to help set him up for success in every way?

Before he comes:

Communicate, communicate, communicate.

Let him know about the excitement that is building. Set up a system if you have to where one elder or deacon contacts him every week the months before and one a day the two weeks before. And then the weeks before every elder either call, text, or e-mail him every day.

Let him know if there are baptisms, good events, anything in the Body there that would encourage him. In two of the churches I went to, the leaders put my address in the bulletin (the address I was moving from) and encouraged the members to write me and tell me about themselves. It was super helpful and I felt I knew a lot about individuals FIRST hand, before I even got there. One lady's letter really stood out. She said something like: "I'm an old lady and I'm told I'm negative at times. I love the Lord and want to go to heaven but it is hard for me not to spot things I don't like and when I do I say something about them in hopes that it can be corrected." Well, as I learned, she certainly knew herself :). But it did help me coming in to know it wasn't personal; she was mean to everyone :).

Supply him with old church bulletins, that's the best history he can get. Be sure to let him know he is not expected to reply to everything sent. After all, he is probably still employed elsewhere.

Welcoming his family:

To quote President Trump, "This is 'uge." How you treat me and welcome me is nice and appreciated, but if you make my wife feel welcomed and my children feel wanted, then you have won a victory with me. So, ask her, would she mind some help unpacking? What meal would you like for your family when you arrive? What can we do that would make the move easier for you? Send her some flowers! Write her a note. Have a child age appropriate gift awaiting the kids in the new location. Remember she is quite probably leaving friends behind and she may not necessarily have even wanted to move. Show her you love her.

I worked with a church where one of the deacons

went around town and got gift cards (several were donated) to some of the local restaurants and presented them to our family when we arrived. That was neat. One church gave my wife a pewter pitcher engraved with the date on it. We don't collect pewter, in fact, at the time it was the only pewter we owned, but the thought was very kind and appreciated. In fact most anything that denotes you have thought about and are excited about this new beginning will be appreciated.

On the day:

First off, remember Sunday is to worship the Lord. Do not forget that. But also remember that His servants are worthy of honor too (Romans 12:10). Don't have "the crazy" guy lead the opening prayer that day. Before the new preacher gets up spend a few minutes introducing him, or interviewing him in front of the church (if appropriate). If you do the interview, ask things about his faith, who influenced him, his strengths, his dreams and hopes, why he wants to preach, any positive connections he might have there. Ask anything that reveals his passion for the church and commitment to the scriptures. Then bring the elders on the stage and pray with/ for him. Lay hands on him, conferring confidence (Acts 13:3). After services take him and his family to lunch or have a potluck. Make it special. This is a big time in the life of a church and not one you want to have over and over and over. Make a big deal of it. He is going to influence the church for a long time.

Write it down:

Remember a month in and three months in to check in with him and his family. Brother Snow regularly would ask about Melanie, Philip, and Andrew just to see how they were months and months after our move. It meant a lot to us. As our friend Jerrie would suggest, throw him a party every few years. You'll be glad you did.

Thanks to Sellers Crain for the idea for this chapter

YOUTH MINISTER INTERVIEW QUESTIONS

- How did you become a Christian?

- What most influenced you spiritually?

- Who has been/is your biggest spiritual influence? Why?

- Why do you want to be a youth minister?

- How long do you plan on being a YM?

- What do you believe to be the job of being a YM? What do you think a YM has to do to get to do what he wants to do?

- Tell me in 4 sentences what you believe about the church?

- Who has authority over you and what does that mean to you?

- Does this apply to both decisions that leadership makes that are more progressive than you are comfortable with as well as those that are more prohibitive than you would like?

-    What do you believe about the "come together" worship of the church?

-    How have you traditionally handled it when you don't get your way?

-    What do you feel the working relationship should be between the rest of the ministry staff and the Youth Minister?

-    What are the 5 favorite things you would most like to do as a Youth Minister for this church?

Part 4
CLOSING THOUGHTS

CONTRACT THOUGHTS

"We are Christians, we don't need no stinkin' contract."

Oh, so you have the gift of divine memory? I'm not sure I remember that one in the 1 Corinthians 12 list, but good for you. For the rest of us, sometimes we forget stuff and it's good that we wrote it down.

Preacher, don't agree to move for less than you can live on. If it looks like that is going to be a problem, don't take the job or write down your expenses and share them.

Elders, consider:
- resources' allowance: books, software, etc
- cell phone if you expect him to use it in the work
- Annual bonus consideration
- Annual cost of living raise
- Staying current in matters of potential conflict. Don't let stuff build up.
- Let him know what meetings he will be invited to and when he will not be included.
- Let know know how you handle criticisms about him and/or his preaching. It will come.
- Make a general rule that short of sin, there

would be no move to dismiss the preacher for one year after a change in eldership. This keeps a guy from being an agenda elder or from being a scapegoat elder.

- Consider a signing bonus; moving can be expensive.
- A Sunday or two between jobs. We've talked about this already. I included it here as a reminder.
- A new computer every 2 to 3 years.
- Consider this possible standard: If you dismiss me I am paid one month severance pay for every year I have been here.

NEGOTIATIONS, YUCK!

"Contract." "Negotiations." They almost sound like dirty words to those of us in ministry. As a result ministers most often end up with pretty raw deals, with little retirement or much to fall back on should they be fired, released or worn out and have to quit.

"Sacrifice." "Dedication." Those are the words that most ministers more readily identify with. So ministers end up "running" huge volunteer organizations with little support and virtually no external authority. And that with almost universal responsibility for the organization's growth, health, and financial burden. If you question that, tell me the last time an eldership was fired for the church not being motivated, not growing, or not reaching its budget. The colossal expectations don't help. Some are expected to grow a congregation that the last five preachers have not been able to grow. And when they make suggestions as to what might help it grow, they are often shut down and shot down.

John Piper didn't help my mind any with the title of his hit book a few years back, "*Brothers,*

We are Not Professionals." And while I understand the concept, we can become such "professionals" that we are white collar, untouchable, never get your hands dirty with ministry hirelings, who are more concerned about making sure we keep our salary and position than about reaching the lost, preaching the challenging truths, or serving and helping the needy. But that represents exactly 0% of the preaching brothers I know! Well, maybe .092%.

On the other hand "a laborer is worthy of his hire" (1 Timothy 5:18, KJV. Note: The NLT translates this, "Those who work deserve their pay!") and many of God's most dedicated servants in the text were not poverty stricken.

I know minster friends of mine who through the years have sacrificed to the point of having nothing at the age when they could no longer work. I know young ministers who live below the poverty line, who work full time and faithfully, yet qualify for food-stamps (of course if they were to apply for them the church would be embarrassed and probably demand they not get them). I've known guys who have gotten them so their family could be fed. The church didn't pay them enough to feed their families but refused to allow them to supplement their salary with a second job, so they would get food stamps but go to the next county to buy groceries so they wouldn't shame the church.

In my own first full time work the prevailing opinion was that I should make less than the lowest paid adult man, so that I could relate to everyone. Incidentally, they didn't appreciate it when I argued that that way I could only relate to one person. The guy who made virtually what I did. They didn't take my happily my "tongue in cheek" suggestion that they pay me a little more than the highest paid man and I could relate all the way up :)!

Brother Clark used to say "our brethren will do better when they know better," and I mostly believe that. Not that I'm the guy to do this, but someone needs to, and maybe if I fire the first volley, somebody will take up where I fail and improve on it. Please do. So here are some thoughts on ministers and compensation:

First to preachers:
1. Don't complain about what you make if you agreed to the compensation you receive. If you don't want what they offer, try to negotiate, if they won't it probably says something about what your working relationship with them is going to be. Note that. But don't as my friend Ronnie says, "poor mouth."

2. If you cannot live on what is offered, go to the leaders, show them what you make and ask them to help you figure it out. They are probably wiser than you are about money and will have some thoughts that may help you.

3. One more to preachers: It is not a sin to move for money. I never see anywhere in the scriptures where that is a sin. But I do see that a man who will not support his family is worse than an infidel.

4. Be prepared to be compared to everyone's favorite former preacher.

Now a couple for the leaders:

1. Try to think about the preacher's family as your own children if possible. As we've asked twice before: Would you want your son or son-in-law to make that amount? If you'd consider it an insult, it probably is. Would you want your grandchild to have that little to live on? Now, I know you started making less than that, but get real, that was 40 years ago.

2. If you WANT to pay your minister more but don't see how it can be done, or if you are hiring a guy and the amount he needs is a little away from what you can pay, go before the church: say, "We are $1,000 or $5,000 apart from getting the man the leaders believe we need. We need 20 of you to give $1 a week more or we need 20 of you to give $5 a week more to bring him here."

3. Give the guy a raise! The first person I heard say

this was Jerrie Barber. If you do not give a cost of living raise then you are saying he is worth less to you than the year before. If you do that to me 3 years straight I'm going to get the message that you must not be pleased with my work.

4. Try to avoid comparisons: Celebrate what you have. There's probably a reason you couldn't get Gus Nichols to come there.

Now a few general tips:

1. While working on a contract, TALK. Work together. Be Christian but discuss it more than 30 seconds. Find out why they think you should make that amount. Find out why he can't come for that amount.

2. Build in incentives to stay: Don't hire a guy who you don't think you want to have around 5 to 10 years. Most every study I've heard says our most fruitful years with a church come after 7 years. Here's some ideas:

   a. Give him a signing bonus: You've probably been without a preacher for a month or two. Take some of that money and let the guy pay down some debt or put some more in his retirement.

   b. Give him incentives to stay: After 5 years we will give you a $5,000.00 bonus. After 10 years we will give you a $10,000.00 bonus. That will make a good preacher think twice before moving. After 15 years we will pay 25% of your existing mortgage off. Do something that makes him think before him moves easily. It is worth it to you as well as to him.

c. *Give him some time off:* Find out when your lowest attendance days are and offer him one or two of those days away.

d. *After a set period of time give him some sort of sabbatical.* I contend that nothing is as emotionally taxing as ministry. You are on 24/7 and have to be available. You are expected to always be at your best. A counselor has to hear everybody's problems but she leaves them at the office. It's a job. In ministry it is a soul and he can't set it aside if there is a problem. He carries the burden that there is ALWAYS someone shooting at him. Always. He carries the burden that he is always one word, one sentence, one sermon away from being fired. I have known guys so burned out they can't "perform" and the church wonders where their fire has gone. I have known guys who moved when a two-month paid sabbatical would have rejuvenated them, but they would not ask for the time away.

Finally, obey Romans 13:7. Honor his good work. Way too many churches are afraid to give honor: afraid they will offend the person who doesn't like the minister (they won't), afraid he will get the "big head" (he won't). Let him know openly you are glad he is your minister. In a good relationship, he will feel honored to be your preacher and you should feel honored that he is yours. You should both feel blessed above the other that you have each other. I don't know how many guys I've heard say: "I just wish they'd say, 'we're glad you're our preacher.'" The truth is I've said it myself, often. Your preacher doesn't do what he does for that reason, but it sure would be nice to hear now and then that the elders are noticing the effort, especially if it is sincerely appreciated.

It is always nice to be loved and appreciated. We are human and we wonder if we will still have a role in this place we call Family next month or year. We wonder why there is no notice of our successes but high notice of our faults. We wonder if the church would hire us again given the chance? We do not do this for praise of men. If we did we would have quit a long time ago. But it is nice for our efforts to be appreciated. And, preacher, if you are blessed (as I am) to work with a church that loves you, let them know you appreciate and love them back.

Melanie and I have had a great week away from local work this week, but not away from God's Work. We spent the week with our sons and daughter-in-laws and LUCAS (just so you know, I wrote this before HOLLEY and MAMIE GRACE came along)! It was awesome in every way. I am deeply in love with these six people. They are the souls of my greatest concern. This week Mel and I celebrated 30 years of marriage. It was so very special to do so with our kids. And Lucas, where to start. He's at that awesome time of walking and beginning to babble. He has this smile that lights up our world and a laugh that is infectious and I could enjoy all day. He's happy and healthy and just as wonderful as can be. Our Laura wrote this back at the first of last year and gave me permission to publish it here. I've waited until the right time and after this week, it seems right. I am proud of her and all of our kids.

WHAT'S YOUR MINISTRY?
Laura Manning Jenkins

Many youth ministers' wives have asked me this question lately: "How do you do it all?" I have had the same question. I normally answer with "You don't. You do what's right for your family and what is most pleasing to God."

Being a minister's wife is hard for soooo many reasons. I remember my mother-in-law saying this after I had Lucas: "I had to decide what I did because I was a Christian and what I did because I was a minister's wife." That statement stuck with me. I have thought about it over and over. So....

What's your ministry? Over the past 7 months this question has reigned over and over in my head. What's my ministry? My ministry used to be very clear. After all, I married a youth minister! My ministry didn't only encompass youth, but youth (specifically our youth group) was the biggest part of my ministry.

As we first started into ministry it felt like a heavy burden. We were ALWAYS on the go. Life seemed to only get faster and faster. I worked two jobs. I was a social worker and a youth minister (although no one would dare call me that :). There were summer days that I would be so tired from a long drive and trying to help my clients that I did not think I could possibly go on and do youth activities that night. However, I LOVED those kids and would have done anything for them. I also love my husband and wanted to spend time him. So I went.

Our first years in ministry literally made me sick. I needed to rest. I needed to take care of myself. I didn't.

Then we moved. I thought that moving to a small town would slow things down. I was wrong. Life only got faster. I went back to school, started an internship, and (again) became a youth minister (alongside my husband). I fell in love with another church, another youth group, and another church family.

Life was good. Life was hard. Things happened. New opportunities arose. We moved again.

This move meant a lot of things. It meant being back with family. It meant being back "home." It meant time to have children. It meant a new job, a new ministry, and a new church family. At the time I had no idea what these things really meant.

This time life spun into a totally different direction. And while I have never known more joy, love, and happiness, I have also never been more confused, more lonely, or more tired. See, while my ministry is still a youth group, my husband, and my counseling, my biggest ministry is now a precious (almost) 7 month old.

This has definitely been the hardest ministry and the biggest responsibility yet. I have never loved a ministry so much, nor been so afraid of it. I see day after day children who are not faithful, who do not feel loved, whose parents have messed up... messed up big. I don't want to be that parent.

But here's the truth. I will mess up. I will need forgiveness. There is no tougher ministry than being a parent. I respect good parenting more than I ever have. I respect the parents who actually parent. I respect the parents that have faithful children.

So in saying all of that, ministry has changed a lot for me. I have had to back out of a lot of youth activities. I have had to change my entire life and the way I did things.

It's been hard. It's been wonderful. It's been tiring. It's been challenging. And at the end of the day...my cup still runneth over. Lucas will always know he is loved and that we walk in the light. He will know our God. He will know goodness, peace, love, mercy, and grace. He will see Christ through us.That is our ministry, because no amount of ministry outside the house makes up for failure at home.

"We MUST learn to live in the Spirit. He has given us exactly what we need to keep us from being mired down with guilt, agitation, and distance from Him. He is providing us full supply for every circumstance, even the hardest, most unexpected ones. He knows, for example, you can't be the mom those kids really need in your own strength, with your own baggage, fulfilling all other obligations that are on you. That's why God has given His Spirit to you—to help you be what you cannot. You are not alone. God's Spirit is with you."
- *Life interrupted, Navigating the Unexpected* by Priscilla Shirer.

A LITTLE PEP TALK

In the first church I ever worked with, I was convinced that if we had more money to do more work, we would grow. Then I moved to another church and the issue was the secretary. If we just had a secretary that was more efficient, we would grow more. At one church, it was an elder that needed to move on or step down. You understand don't you?

You've been there.

What is it with you? A building that is falling apart, a sin that won't be forgotten, a preacher who doesn't seen to have the energy to help? I want to share something with you. I know you didn't do it on purpose, neither did I, but when you say any of the above you are "making" them more powerful and more important than Christ!

It's like saying: "Lord, I know you are powerful but we have this awful building and I just think it is more powerful to affect our church than You are." "God, I know you are Lord of Lords, Ruler of the Universe, but we just don't have the money to advertise like I wish we could and therefore, well, to be frank, that's more powerful than You." You fill in the blank. But be honest. Isn't He able? Isn't He wiser? Isn't He more than whatever you put in the blank? Now, get out there and do the work and let Him give the increase!

But first, consider these verses to reassure you:

Ephesians 1:20-22 - *Christ when he raised him from the dead and seated him at his right hand in the heavenly places, far above all rule and authority and power and dominion, and above every name that is named, not only in this age but also in the one to come. And he put all things under his feet and gave him as head over all things to the church...*

Ephesians 3:20-21 - *Now to him who is able to do far more abundantly than all that we ask or think, according to the power at work within us, to him be glory in the church and in Christ Jesus throughout all generations, forever and ever. Amen.*

Colossians 1:18 - *And he is the head of the body, the church. He is the beginning, the firstborn from the dead, that in everything he might be preeminent.*

Psalm 8:1 - *O LORD, our Lord, how excellent is thy name in all the earth! who hast set thy glory above the heavens.*

Psalm 89:7 - *God greatly to be feared in the council of the holy ones, and awesome above all who are around him?*

Psalm 95:3 – *For the LORD is a great God, and a great King above all gods.*

Psalms 96:4 – *For great is the LORD, and greatly to be praised; he is to be feared above all gods.*

Now, go, do, create, serve, be, make something happen because "he who is in you is greater than he who is in the world!"

A FINAL WORD

To Elders

I see the desperation in your email, I hear it in your voice. "We need help." "If you know of anyone." "We're struggling to find the right guy."

I want to assure you it will be OK. Remember God hears prayer and rewards faith. And I want to assure you we will help anyway we can. Our email address is *TJI@TheJenkinsInstitute.com* and our phone number is (972) 861-2434.

To Ministers

I can't let this book end without saying "thank you" for giving your life to the service of our Lord and His Kingdom. We are for you. We understand the challenges and want you to know we will help you any way we can. Our email address is *TJI@TheJenkinsInstitute.com* and our phone number is (972) 861-2434. Don't hesitate to call, text, or email if we can aid you.

OTHER TITLES AVAILABLE FROM
THE JENKINS INSTITUTE:

His Word (52 weeks of devotionals thru the NT)
The Living Word: Sermons of Jerry A. Jenkins
The Glory of Preaching
Before I Go: Notes from Older Preachers

Thoughts from the Mound
More Thoughts from the Mound
All I Ever Wanted to Do Was Preach
I Hope You Have to Pinch Yourself

The Preacher as Counselor
Don't Quit on a Monday
Don't Quit on a Tuesday

Five Secrets and a Decision
Centered: Marking Your Map in a Muddled World

Me, You, and the People in the Pews
From Mother's Day to Father's Day

A Minister's Heart
A Youth Minister's Heart
A Mother's Heart
A Father's Heart

FREE EVANGELISM RESOURCES BY JERRY JENKINS:
God Speaks Today
Lovingly Leading Men to the Savior

To order, visit *thejenkinsinstitute.com/shop*